The Family Business, The Family Farm

America's Amazing Economic Engine

Edward T. Pendarvis

This book is dedicated to . . .

Elaine, my wonderful wife and partner in life, who took a chance on me, and whose warm and beautiful smile always lifts my heart.

My five wonderful girls: Stephanie Myrick-Pendarvis McDonald, Elizabeth Myrick-Pendarvis Martin, Sara Pendarvis Bazemore, Melany West Warfuel and Jennifer West Shuman. As I have tried to make a living, they have made my life worth living. I am truly a blessed man.

Every Sunbelt office owner that had the courage to join us in this adventure of private business.

The wonderful and talented folks who have added so greatly to this project. Especially to my dear friends Tom and Barbara West, who guided me through this business and this book; Elizabeth Lutyens, my editor, who translated my scribblings into English; Adam Houston of Houston Design, who created the front and back covers; Sue West Levine, who transformed the manuscript into handsome type; and most especially Alison Van Horn, my dear friend and translator whose amazing patience and helpful suggestions were incredibly invaluable. Thank you, thank you, thank you!

v

Contents

Foreword

Behold, I show you a mystery; this book is about YOU, about how you choose to live your life and how you choose to provide for yourself and your family.

It would seem at first to be a book about me and my business; however, I spend my work life trying to help folks make the right decision about how they will earn their living. Basically, you can work for someone else in a job or you can work for yourself in your own business. Both have rewards and both have risk.

With 8,000,000 unemployed people chasing 3,500,000 jobs, plus untold millions who do not like their current job, plus those who are "underemployed" consider this: Provide your own job and your own job security – go into business *for* yourself, but not *by* yourself.

You can do that by buying an existing business with the present owner's help – one that has a proven track record of success, with trained employees, an existing customer base and an immediate cash flow - or you could buy a franchise in a specific industry, with a proven track record of success and the franchisor's help.

I will show you how to do this, how to weigh the options for you and your family and how to purchase a business and protect yourself in the process as best you can. There are no guarantees except that working for someone else is no guarantee either. There is no substitute for common sense, good self-appraisal, due dilligence and human intuition. In business, as in life, you need to use all of the resources that the Good Lord has provided you.

Probably the most important decision you will make in your life is who you are going to marry. I'll leave that one to you. Next to that decision in importance is how to provide for your family and derive an income sufficient to provide for the house payment, car payment, food and education for your children.

In the United States of America, we are FREE to choose our destiny, our work path, where, how and who we will work for. I say work for the man or woman in the mirror. They truly, truly have your best interest at heart and they will not let you down and they won't fire you mid-career.

If you manage your business well and make the necessary investments of time, money and adjustments (course corrections) to provide a product and/or service that the marketplace responds favorably to – you just may have a job for life. Also, you have the possibility of adding great value to the business and the possibility of something to sell later on.

There has never been a better opportunity for going into business for yourself. Now is the time; where you live or want to live, is the place. In this book, I will show you how. I invite you to take this table of contents and write YOUR book. The next day, the next year, the next twenty years are up to you.

Thank you for taking the time to read this book on my thoughts and advice on the real world of small business. My greatest hope is that you will find it beneficial to you in making some business decisions and personal decisions that will significantly help you and your family.

Best wishes and respect . . .

Chapter 1

Believing in the Value of Small Business

Uncertain economic times! Job security is gone; the stock market is a roller coaster; interest on savings accounts barely keeps up with inflation; you can't live on social security. Where do you invest for the short term and where do you invest for the long haul?

I say, " Invest in a sure thing- invest in yourself!"

Go into business for yourself and provide for your own job security, income, and retirement. These are important accomplishments all within your reach.

1. *Job Security:* You own your own business and therefore you have a job for life. You are not subject to being laid off or downsized in mid-career through no fault of your own.

2. *Income Potential:* When you take a salaried job for a certain amount of money, that is all you are going to make no matter how hard or how smart you work. When you work for yourself, you have no guarantees; however, you also have no limits on your income. You may be able to make more money, especially considering the fact that a majority of big businesses started off as small businesses.

3. *Retirement Program:* As you build and grow your business, you are building and growing a valuable asset that you should be able to sell when you wish to retire, and the sale of your business could produce your retirement program. You may also be able to provide jobs for others, especially your children or other family members. Compare this situation to that of a salaried employee. Employees cannot "sell" their jobs.

When you stop to think about it, what do you need out of a job or a business? You need to earn a living, an income to provide for yourself and your family. I have no doubt that the best way to accomplish and perhaps even surpass that goal is to own your own business. I will devote the next few chapters to pleading my case for that proposition. You will be the judge and jury - and as one should do with all cases - I will ask you to keep an open mind until you have heard and weighed all the evidence.

This book is based on facts, feelings, experience and information that I have garnered and absorbed as a student of business and as a teacher of business brokerage to thousands of new business brokers and seminar attendees over the last twenty years.

One of the things I find fascinating about education is that you can give away all of your knowledge thousands of times, and you will still have just as much as when you started. Actually, you have more, because you always learn from your students. Most of my assumptions are based on life's experiences, good and bad; and on business experiences, successful and unsuccessful; and on my study of the real world of other businesses and other business owners. I find their life stories and their business stories fascinating, as well as encouraging: all successful people also have had many, many failures.

I feel that we probably learn more from our failures than we do from our successes. And by the way, if you have never failed at anything in your life – stick around. Life and the Lord have a way of leveling the playing field in all of our lives and that usually means some successes and some "not so successes." The latter circumstance gives us opportunities to make "course corrections" as we go through life and especially business life. In my experience, business life is a continuous stream of "course corrections."

I am a rather simple man, and I will use simple explanations and examples to present my theories on business and to convey the real value of a business to you as an individual, as a family member, and as a community constituent. You will find, however simple, that my "rules" do apply, and as in most games it's the basic, everyday "blocking and tackling" that ultimately help you succeed or win.

Having had the pleasure and challenge of founding and developing, along with some wonderful partners, the world's largest business brokerage franchise, I have seen some interesting business transactions as well as some interesting sellers and buyers. At Sunbelt, with over 1500 active brokers in 300 plus locations in the United States and 11 foreign countries, we have over 10,000 businesses listed for sale and deal with over 250,000 potential buyers per year.

Since 1982, I have personally sold or helped manage the sale of over 1000 small businesses. Now, the Sunbelt Network as a whole sells over 1000 businesses every 3 or 4 months. Each business transaction has a very important seller and a very important buyer who are trying to accomplish some very important objectives for themselves and their families. All of them are trying to do the best possible job to accomplish their goals through the sale and/or purchase. Now it's your turn! Getting you as a buyer or you as a seller to your personal goal line is the theme that drives this book.

You will find that most business sales progress three yards, two yards, five more yards and then a first down. Then four yards, three yards, four more yards and another first down. There are very few ninety-nine yard runs or "Hail Mary" passes in the real world of business brokerage. However, when we get the buyer to his or her goal line we also just got the seller to his or her goal line and guess what? It is the very same goal line, and all teams win. Buying and selling a business should not be an adversarial transaction.

A business deal has to work for the buyer or he or she will not buy. Likewise, it has to work for the seller or he or she will not sell. It truly, truly has to be a win-win situation or the transaction will not close. Furthermore, when I get the buyer and seller to their goal line, I've also managed to get myself, the business broker, to my own goal line. So it actually is a win-win-win situation!

This book is not based on academic theory. You will not find this information in any self-help manual, in any business school or university curriculum, and certainly not at the Small Business Administration. Amazingly, even the latter knows very little about the "real world" of small business. It is perplexing to me that 98 percent of businesses in America are small business, yet all of our government and educational programs are focused on and geared towards preparing students for getting a job with or managing a big business.

We have educated five generations of Americans to "get a job" with big business; however, over the last ten years the job market has shrunk and continues to do so. Big business has laid off hundreds of thousands of people through reengineering, downsizing or rightsizing, and most of all the job growth has been in small business. Since big business and small business are two entirely different animals, I'll show you some of these critical differences and how they affect you in earning your living. This information is "stuff" that has been acquired over a lifetime of observing the dealings of small business and most of which you will not learn in college. Although many fine colleges and universities have initiated programs and curricula built around entrepreneurship and are doing a great job teaching the basics, most topics still deal only with "big business rules."

I feel that this book will provide you the information necessary to look at the real world of small business ownership and understand small business value from a "street-smart" perspective.

Armed and fortified with this real world information, you will be a more educated and knowledgeable buyer and/or seller. I have always found that the more educated and knowledgeable my clients and customers are, the better chance I have of helping them get to their goal line.

Now remember, I am a self-proclaimed simple man, so I like to break things down into basic examples and formulas on which to build a solid foundation from which both the buyer and seller can take the all-important leap of faith. Buying and/or selling a business *is* a leap of faith for both parties. There are no solid guarantees in business, just as there are no solid guarantees in life.

There are no guarantees in marriage, in having and raising children, in sports, in investments, in health, in taking a job or in buying a business. To make an educated decision, you gather your best information, seek the best professional advice, do all the necessary and available due diligence, say a prayer or lots of prayers, make the best decision you can, take a deep breath and step out onto that precipice. Take the leap - who knows, you may accomplish your basic goals of earning a living, and you just might be successful beyond your wildest dreams.

Either way, you are choosing a path walked before you by virtually every successful businessman or businesswoman, from Henry Ford, George Eastman, Ray Krock, Col. Harland Sanders, Dave Thomas, Sam Walton, Ted Turner, Michael Dell, to Bill Gates and Martha Stewart (before the stock sale). They all started out with a small business and something they believed in and through a series of hard work, more hard work and constant course corrections (and perhaps some divine intervention and a little luck) they built businesses that produce products and/or services that the marketplace responded to. So can you.

Two things that these winners had in common were (1), they liked what they were doing, and (2), they owned their own business. It is almost impossible to be very successful in business if these two ingredients are not present.

Have you ever seen a successful athlete who did not like the sport he or she was playing? Have you ever seen a successful actor or singer who didn't like being an actor or a singer; or a successful doctor, lawyer or businessman who did not like their profession? Do you think that they became successful and *then* liked what they were doing, or the other way around? I vote on the latter.

If you line up what you like to do with what makes you money, you just might hit a home run. At the very least, you'll enjoy your work. It's still work, it's not play, but *liking* gives you a much better chance of putting that extra something into your business that makes it hugely successful.

A stand-up comic on the college campus in the early 1960s by the name of Brother Dave Garner used to offer this funny little line: "Don't tell me none of your doubts, man, I've got enough doubts of my own. Tell Me Something You Believe In."

Well, I believe in the value of small business to you and to America today, more than ever. I believe that small business is the best way to provide a living for you and your family and also to provide you with job security. I believe that owning your own business offers you far and away the best opportunity to become a millionaire if you wish to. No other investment opportunity comes close. I believe that small business has provided virtually all of the job growth in the United States over the last decade.

I also believe that small business owners are the true American heroes in that they make our communities, therefore our country, work. Small business owners own and operate the local businesses that provide the goods and services that add to the richness of our life every day. These owners get up each morning, usually before sunrise, go to work and open the local dry cleaners, the restaurants, the retail stores, the auto repair shops, the convenience stores, the drugstores, the coin laundries, the small manufacturing companies, the distributors, the local bars where, like Cheers, "everybody knows your name." They are the doctors, lawyers, preachers, real estate brokers, business brokers, consultants, and owners of beauty shops. They provide jobs for anywhere from one to twenty other folks, and they meet payroll every Friday. They take care of their families and they add significant value to our lives and help make our communities work. They are on every side of the road (and every side road), and there are approximately 20 million of them.

These business owners support their families, schools, churches and government by means of their own business. They are our neighbors; they are always there. You see them everyday. You can count on them and, in return, they can count on you as a customer and perhaps as a friend.

CNN took a poll in 2000 asking, "Who do you trust the most?" Not surprisingly, the government and big business scored only 4 percent each on the "Trust Meter" (and this was before the Enron and Worldcom disasters). The Supreme Court ranked the highest with 44 percent; however, running a close second at 33% was Small Business. They are our neighbors, we know them and they know us. We trust each other.

Small business is America's Amazing Economic Engine, and I'll show you how it can work for you. I'll also show you how to look at its real value and how to go about finding the right business for you and your family. We'll also cover how to buy the business at the right price, on terms and conditions that work for you and how to protect your best interests in the process.

I hope you will find this book beneficial in building a solid foundation from which you take your "leap of faith" and – if you allow me to mix my metaphors - gain a slice of the "American Pie" for yourself. It just may provide you and your family nourishment for today, for tomorrow and for many generations to come. When you own your own business, you are investing your time and money in a sure thing; you are investing in *yourself*!

Chapter 2
My Job as a Man (Provider)

My job as a man (provider) is to provide for the needs of my wife and children and to provide for them a good name. To do that, I need to derive an income from a job or a family business or a family farm that provides for our material and financial needs and allows us to live honorably.

I will leave the task of defining "living honorably" to folks far more qualified than I am and I will attempt to talk about what I know a little something about, family businesses and family farms.

I am fifty-eight years old and have been working in family businesses and also on family farms since I was nine. At one time or another, I have owned a construction company, a real estate company, a restaurant, a night club, a band, a small manufacturing company, a small distribution business and a convenience store. I've just about always owned my own business and worked for myself. Since 1982, I have been *selling* family businesses in Charleston, South Carolina. Over that time, I've sold or managed the sale of small businesses in almost every kind of industry, including retail, service, manufacturing, distribution, restaurants, lounges, coin laundries, liquor stores and convenience stores, and franchises of all sorts, all of which were family businesses.

My business is selling businesses, or business brokerage, and the more you know about your business (or field), the more comfortable you are with it. When I started twenty years ago, most folks had never heard of a business broker, myself included. One of my main hopes in writing this book is that it will help you understand the real value of small business to you and to all of us, because America is moving back to small business in a huge way. History tends to repeat itself and more and more folks are going back to self-employment to provide their living. My life mirrors that.

I grew up in a small town in lower South Carolina, called Allendale, about ninety miles west of Charleston. Everyone in that town in the 1950s either owned a small family business or a family farm, or worked for someone who did. There were no "big businesses" in Allendale, and there still aren't. My father and all the folks I knew provided for their families by owning and operating their own business or farm. Although I didn't realize it at the time, that lifestyle was a great education and training ground for one of the most exciting and needed businesses in America today, selling businesses (business brokerage).

Basically, you can work for someone else or you can work for yourself; one way or another you have to make a living. My suggestion is that it is best, although not always easiest, to work for yourself, and that means owning your own business (farm).

Actually, when you think about it, a family business is a family farm. You have to own it, decide what you're going to plant, prepare to plant, plant at the right time, nurture, fertilize and maintain the crop, keep the weeds and pests at bay, pray for proper weather, harvest and go to market at the right time, and hope that the market wants or needs and will pay for your crop. Not to mention the struggles to make more income than it cost you to produce the crop.

Also, without openly wishing for locusts, droughts, floods, or other adversity on your fellow farmers, you can only hope that your market is not ruined by overproduction of your product, service or crop. As we all know, competition is healthy just so long as you can stay ahead of it.

In a family business, you not only have to provide a product or service that the marketplace wants or needs and will pay for, you have to manage your business so that it produces more than it costs to operate. You also, as just stated above, have to watch for the competition. Hopefully, the business provides for you and your family's material and financial needs - and a good name by virtue of a "farm" managed in a way that contributes positively to the community.

As I have had the opportunity to help my partners grow our business brokerage business, Sunbelt Business Brokers Network, Inc., to be the largest business brokerage franchise in the world, I've had the chance to travel all across America many times by plane, train, bus and automobile. Since I do the entire initial broker training for Sunbelt, every week since we started franchising in 1993, I've traveled to a major city in the United States to conduct broker training. Every week I go either to Atlanta, Orlando, New Orleans, Washington D.C., New York, Chicago, Minneapolis, Dallas, Houston, Denver, Phoenix, Los Angeles, San Francisco, Portland or Seattle. By training in one of these cities every week, I travel back across the country every 90 days. During these journeys, I have had "windshield time" and "airport time" to put together ideas about the world of business. I have gained a healthy respect for my fellow "Road Warriors" whose jobs require a lot of travel. I have truly become a "Roads Scholar." While traveling and learning about the various businesses and people that exist in these cities, I've had the chance to study the history of many big businesses that started as small businesses, and I have had the chance to study the stories about the founders. I've been to Corbin, Kentucky, where Col. Harland Sanders started Kentucky Fried Chicken; to the original

Wendy's in Columbus, Ohio, started by Dave Thomas; to the home of Mr. George Eastman of Eastman Kodak in Rochester, New York; to Moline, Illinois, the home of John Deere; and out to a small town in Northwest Arkansas called Bentonville to the original Walton's 5&10, the home of Wal-Mart, the largest retailer in the world.

Bentonville is about 15 miles from Lowell, Arkansas, home of J.B. Hunt Trucking, the country's largest trucking company, and 20 miles away from Springdale, Arkansas, the home of Tyson Foods, the world's largest chicken company.

I have also been to Atlanta, the "capitol of the South," where Ted Turner came up with some wild and crazy ideas about a twenty-four hour news service on cable television, later to become CNN, and also bought a mediocre baseball team called the Atlanta Braves with the equally crazy notion of making them "America's Team." And what about his nutty scheme to buy all of those old films at MGM: who's ever going to watch classic movies? Next he'll probably try to get folks to eat buffalo.

The point I am trying to make is that almost all big businesses started off as a small business, and somehow hit the market right. Many of them began in small towns and cities across the United States. I find the stories - of both the businesses and their owners - fascinating; they are an integral part of the American business history – the essence of what I call America's Real and Amazing Economic Engine.

Let's explore some of the changes, small and large, in the world of business and in the world of work that have occurred and see how those changes effect our present and will affect our future.

There are millions of American Business Heroes (small business owners) who provide for themselves and their families and provide jobs for millions more. In fact, in the last decade substantially all of the new job growth has been in small business, while big business continues laying folks off by the tens of thousands.

In 1999, a new program appeared on TV called "Who Wants to be a Millionaire?" Well, apparently, and not unexpectedly, just about everyone does. There are a lot of books out about how to become a millionaire, most of them "investment advice driven," to entice regular folks to invest in the stock market, real estate or precious metals. I have always found it interesting that all of those books have one phrase in common, "The best way to become a millionaire, *except by owning your own business,*" is this way or that way. They all have that exception stated somewhere in the beginning of the text.

This is kind of like saying, "Except for Michael Jordan, who's the best basketball player in history?" If you don't exclude him, Michael Jordan would be everyone's answer. The same is true of the best way to become a millionaire. Own your own business and be in business for yourself; no other method comes close.

Now, most of us will not get to be millionaires; however, we do all have that chance. You will not get to be a millionaire by working for someone else, unless of course, you have saved fifty to one hundred dollars per month religiously since you were twenty years old and invested it at seven percent interest compounded and never touched it until you were sixty-five. Sorry I missed out on that opportunity! I'm already fifty-eight, and over the last year we all relearned that investments in the stock market can go down just as they can go up.

You have no doubt noticed that I use the terms family farm and family business interchangeably. I do this because, essentially, their function is the same. That function is to provide for the needs of the owner's family materially and financially. In the world of work, you can work for yourself or you can work for someone else; the needed result is the same, you *must* have an income. You must have an income so you can pay the house payment, car payment, electric and telephone bills, feed, clothe and educate your children. You know what I have noticed; children all want to eat at least three times a day; everyday, yesterday, today and tomorrow and girls always need new clothes.

Consequently, I believe that you are better off going into business for yourself and working as hard and as smart as you can, using your own learned and God-given talents and abilities to develop a business that provides a service and/or product to which the market responds. You will also provide for your own job security, something that has "Gone with the Wind" in American big business. You may end up with a business of considerable value to sell when you finally retire, and who knows, you might get to be a millionaire.

In writing a book or giving a speech, I use what I learned at my Dale Carnegie course in 1970 - it is best to write or talk about what you know. I've always heard that it should be interesting, informative, entertaining and brief. Well, I find life interesting, informative, entertaining and brief. Hopefully this book will also follow that formula. I am not sure what I know about the world of work or about being a man, husband, or father except the observations and experiences that I have had.

In sharing these observations with you, I hope that they may be of some help to you as we look at the changes and similarities in the world of business and the world of work in America during the twentieth century and as we prepare for how we'll provide for our families in the twenty-first century. We'll explore some of the changes, small and large, in the world of work that have occurred and how those changes have affected and continue to affect us all.

In America, we have educated five generations about how to "get a job" and to develop a job skill or management skill to become more marketable. Not surprisingly, after a layoff by a major corporation or the government, special job training or retraining will be offered to help you get another job. A job, by the way, that you could be laid off from again a few years down the road. Maybe just trading one job for another is not the best answer.

I believe you are better off working for yourself, and if you are going into business for yourself, I believe with all my heart that you are better off buying an existing business or a franchise with a proven track record of success than you are starting your business from scratch.

United States Department of Commerce statistics show that 65-90 percent of start-up businesses are not still in business after 5 years. On the other hand, 90-95 percent of existing businesses that have been in business 3 years or longer with a successful track record or a franchise with a successful track record are still in business after 5 years. Now, is that a turn around of risk or what?

I will show you why those statistics are true and explain how to find the right business for you, as well as how to buy it. Also, even with the tremendous changes in the world of work and technology in the last few years, I'll show you how the more things change, the more they stay the same.

Just as I treat "farm" and "business" interchangeably, so do I write about my personal life and my business life: they are one and the same. Every decision I make affects the people closest to me - my family - and no reflection upon my business experience would be complete without including them. I am a small businessman and, as such, I need and fortunately have a supportive and understanding partner in life in my wife, Elaine. Through her support and patience, and with the Lord's help, we have been successful in blending my three daughters, her two daughters, my two ex-wives and two husbands-in-law into a strong family unit. Elaine has done her part - *and* my part - in so many important family events when business required that I be away. I thank her for her love and support and together we make up a whole family team. My family; immediate and extended, are an integral and wonderful part of my story as they will be with your story. Realizing that, let's look at the world of work in the early twentieth century.

Chapter 3

The World of Work from 1900 to Present

The United States of America is a big country and the Lord has blessed her with natural resources and a diverse and varied population made up of all nationalities, races, creeds, religions and skills. In the early twentieth century, most folks lived and worked in small towns, on small farms, or in small businesses owned and run by citizens of that town. The entrepreneurial spirit was strong in America.

A normal family unit had a father who worked for himself or worked for someone else to provide an income for the family, and usually the wife worked inside the home providing for the needs of her husband and children. One-income families were the norm.

The beginning of the Industrial Revolution in the late 1800s and the advent of America's involvement in World War I heralded a major transformation in the world of work. The development of giant factories that produced steel, railroads and automobiles, fuel, steamships, telephones, large retailers and electricity brought a "sea change" in the way we provide for our family income. A man could make more by working for someone else, particularly a big company, than he could working for himself. The "Big Company," or the Industrial Age, had begun.

At the turn of the century, we were a nation of small farms and shopkeepers; however, the world of work was about to change forever. Men started leaving the farms and small towns and going to big cities to work for a big company for wages that far exceeded what they could make in a small business or farm.

These cities and factories began to grow up around transportation hubs of rivers, seaports or railheads, and folks migrated to the cities and to the jobs. The "work" mission remained the same, however, to provide for the needs of the family.

As the companies grew to fill the needs of the market for products and services, so did the needs for capital and for management to supply the needs of growth within the companies. Company management changes were necessary to manage the resulting large companies. John D. Rockefeller's Standard Oil Company developed the modern managerial organization wherein the company had jobs to be filled in "Organizational Charts," and for the first time the job defined the worker rather than the worker defining the job.

After WWI, the banking industry and the new stock market, or equities market, was straining to keep up with the explosive growth of manufacturers, retailers, transportation, fuel, communications and utilities and to address the markets created by the demands of such a robust economy. Everybody became investors and began dreaming of getting rich in the stock market. Continuous investments by an excess of buyers drove the prices of stocks up and up, rather than their market price being based on the actual value of the companies the folks were investing in.

Sure enough, the bubble burst. The stock market crashed in 1929, and the Great Depression began and permeated throughout the entire nation, impacting virtually every American family and citizen in some way. Unemployment, for the first time, became a major disaster to the family when those thousands of men who wanted and needed to work couldn't find gainful employment. Almost one third of the employable population was unemployed; many lined up in soup kitchens and others (hobos, we called them) went from town to town searching for work.

Folks who worked for themselves in small business and on small farms were still employed and fared better. They still had their jobs, since they worked for themselves.

For the first time, the Federal government became directly involved in the economy and in the providing of jobs with FDR's WPA (Work Program Administration), and Congress passed laws that provided for social security and unemployment insurance and certain other areas of welfare. These programs provided somewhat of a security net to help provide for families and individuals in need, which means all of us at some point or another in our lifetimes.

These measures and the onset of World War II brought America out of the depression and put everyone back to work in factories, transportation, the military, retailing, distribution, fuel, communications and utilities. For the first time, women in large numbers went to work outside the home to help meet the needs of a country at war, as well as the needs of their families. America, the American family, and the world of work were again changed forever.

The post-war economy was growing stronger and stronger, and with the G.I. Bill, thousands of veterans were going back to school and to college to further their education and make themselves more valuable in the job market.

Families were buying their own homes with government loans from the Federal Housing Administration (FHA) or Veterans Administration (VA), and the American suburbs were developed. Everyone wanted a home with a yard, and of course, that was the best of all worlds (a family farm - or yard - with a job and income instead of crops). The quality of life was significantly improved for millions of Americans. The hours of the typical job (eight hours a day, forty hours a week) were better than working for yourself, and the job produced a good, livable wage without worrying so much about complete management of the company and the other workers. The wages, especially as established with a floor, or "minimum" wage, allowed for a higher standard of living than could be obtained by working for oneself or farming, and the "Great American Middle Class" was born.

Consumerism was *in*! We all wanted a house, one or two cars, a dishwasher, washing machine and dryer, college education for our children, two-week vacations - and television.

Much to the nation's delight, television was invented and developed to bring entertainment and news to America, and as it became available to a mass market, our world became much smaller once we had this wonderful talking picture box right in our own homes. Television changed our world, and as with most aspects of life, there was some good and some bad in those changes. Basically, America in the 1950s was just as it was depicted on TV. Father had a job with a livable wage, Mother ran the house and children, the children were getting an education and eating three times a day, and the three major television networks (ABC, NBC and CBS) signed off the air with the National Anthem at 11:00 pm, sending Americans to sleep. How things change!

The 1960s arrived quietly enough. Most Americans had a good job or worked for themselves, and life seemed to be going pretty well. Big companies were getting even bigger and providing more and more jobs. A young person's goal was to get a good education and get a good job with a big name company. If he performed his job well with the big company, that was his "job security," and he would stay with the company, possibly in the same position, through retirement. If he was good, he might even move up the corporate ladder of success, and at some point retire as an executive or at least retire as a former employee with some stream of retirement income from the big company.

Like a lot of things that seem too good to last, that image of America was about to unravel. Women, African Americans and other minorities were not sharing in the American Dream. The civil rights movement of the 1960s awoke the nation and as a result, many, but certainly not all, wrongs slowly began to be righted. Regarding race issues, the grossly false "separate but equal" programs were exposed for being anything but equal, and eventually opportunities for education, jobs, housing and advancement were available to all Americans.

In the 1960s, our country was also rocked by the assassination of our President, John F. Kennedy, followed by the assassination of Dr. Martin Luther King, Jr., the civil rights leader, and Senator Robert Kennedy, a candidate for President. No one who lived through that time remained untouched by those events. Many can remember where they were and what they were doing when the tragedies occurred.

America's military involvement in Vietnam, a little known country in Southeast Asia, escalated from an advisory role to a full-scale but undeclared war involving over one million of our finest young people as we tried to prevent a supposed "domino effect" - the spread of communism throughout the Asian world. After fourteen years of indecisiveness and the tragic loss of millions of lives, including more than 58,000 Americans, we finally pulled out of South Vietnam, vowing never again to send our young heroes back to war without knowing why we were there.

The 1970s saw a President, Richard Nixon, resign to avoid impeachment in what was dubbed the Watergate affair. We struggled to regain our footings in what had been the American way, and failing that, just get back to a normal life in a stable and peaceful world. Our absolute trust in government, however, was damaged forever.

We continued to move to the cities as small farms were lost to development and were unable to compete with large "corporate farms" that were run by management teams with lots of capital. Small businesses also had a difficult time competing with big corporate businesses which were encroaching on small business territory and competing more and more for the same customers. The world of work and small business was changing yet again.

Until now most big businesses were in manufacturing, retailing, distribution, transportation, government contracting, oil, utilities, communications and - in cities - television. Small towns and suburbs were safe havens for small business retailers and service providers who owned and operated their own business. Gas station owner/operators represented big companies on-site, and financing was done by local banks (banks were not allowed to cross state lines). Automobile companies like General Motors, Ford and Chrysler had "local" dealers who were small business people. Consequently, in many ways, big business and small business had somewhat of a partnership, and each had its own defined role and location in the marketplace.

Giant retailers began to creep into the suburbs of large cities with the development of shopping centers and shopping malls that were following the market of customers as they migrated from urban areas to suburbia. Sears, Montgomery Ward, J.C. Penney, and a discount retailer named Kmart began aggressively moving into the suburbs, creating shopping districts and providing opportunities for small support businesses such as card shops, gift shops, restaurants, hair salons and dry cleaners.

In order to "keep up with the Joneses'" standard of living, more and more families started to have the wife seek employment outside of the home, and two family incomes became the norm, rather than the exception. "Traditional" women's jobs such as teaching, health care and secretarial support began to give way to women becoming business executives, doctors, lawyers and business owners.

Once women got a taste of their own income and independence, there was no turning back. Today women are involved successfully and positively in all aspects of business and in many professions, even the military. In fact, women are doing an outstanding job, even at such male bastions as The Citadel, the military college of South Carolina. Contrary to popular belief in Charleston at the time, the walls did not fall down when women were admitted. (Since I am a 1965 graduate of The Citadel, I feel able to comment with some authority!)

Two more major changes were developing in America that would have a revolutionary impact on the world of business and work. A milkshake appliance salesman named Ray Krock and a nice retired motel owner and restaurateur from Corbin, Kentucky, who had a chicken recipe that everyone loved, started a fast food phenomenon that led to a business revolution called *franchising*. The phenomenon of franchising is still having a major impact on the world of work and allowing a lot of folks to go back into business "for themselves but not by themselves."

The second major change started in a small town in Arkansas slightly northwest of the Ozark Mountains with a store named Walton's 5&10. Although the town of Bentonville is still only about 10,000 in population, the company, Wal-Mart, is the largest retailer in the world with over 220 billion in annual sales. It has over 4380 stores, employs over 1.28 million people and has had a major impact on work and small business in virtually every city and town in America and the world. Recently, Wal-Mart surpassed General Motors as the company having the highest gross sales in the world. Only Exxon-Mobile had higher gross sales, and in 2001 Wal-Mart overtook them as well.

Add a few of the other major, aggressive retailers like Home Depot, Lowes, Staples, Office Depot, The Limited, Gap and franchises or multiple outlet stores like McDonald's, Burger King, Subway, Taco Bell, Applebee's, Chili's, Olive Garden, Ruby Tuesdays, TGI Fridays, Pep Boys, Precision Tune, Ammco Transmission, One Hour Martinizing, Fast Signs, Deck the Walls, etc., etc. and you will see how big business and franchising have permeated every aspect of business, large and small, in towns large and small across America.

Another quantum leap that has greatly impacted our world is the advancement of technology. Now it is possible to watch television 24 hours a day, choosing from a menu of hundreds of channels. Further, and perhaps the biggest of all modern developments are personal computers, the Internet, and the World Wide Web. Wow!!! We've just begun to see the changes in the world of work that technology will produce and/or demand. Every business around the globe will be affected by this technology; indeed; the richest folks in America today are a result of these changes in technology and the response of the marketplace to them.

With the 1980s came a robust economy and, as big business sought ways to compete and succeed in a fast changing world, a new management phenomenon was born called "reengineering," "downsizing" or "rightsizing," which are terms that have become the code-word for "firing" people or, more appropriately, if you're one of the tens of thousands of folks that have been "downsized," the literal translation is, "You ain't got a job anymore."

Now it's a little more complicated than that, of course, but the net results are the same - for the first time in some people's adult lives, they don't have a job and the idea that "if you got a good job with a big company and you did a good job, that was your job security and you'd work with that company until retirement" is a concept that is gone forever. When was the last time you heard the phrase "move up the corporate ladder"?

One thing that makes this change so personal and disconcerting is that it doesn't matter how good a job you've done, when the company merges, reengineers or is acquired by another company, you might expect to hear what Ted Turner told his son, who was working for CNN at the time it was acquired by Time-Warner and was hoping to stay on after the merger: "Son, you're toast."

The world of work has been turned upside down in America - job security is gone and is not coming back. This is another sea change in the world of work. It is just as big as the Industrial Revolution's impact was on the 19th and 20th centuries, only in reverse. A good lesson for dealing with some of these changes can be found in Dr. Spencer Johnson's excellent book, *Who Moved My Cheese?*.

Across America the work place has eliminated hundreds of thousands of jobs – over 1.8 million in 2001 alone. Educated, experienced people who want to work and need to work are unemployed for the first time in their adult lives. Their "American Dream Job" is gone and will remain gone. Now that the income from the job has stopped, guess what has not stopped - the house payment, car payments, the children's education bills - everyone still wants to eat three times a day.

Think back with me a few years. If you find a dictionary over eleven years old, the words reengineering, downsizing and rightsizing are not included. Prior to eleven years ago, if a major company had announced that they were laying off 10,000 of their key people, what would happen to their stock? It would have *dropped like a rock*, devastating the company and the community as well as the 10,000 people who were laid off. Since reengineering, the stock market reaction to a layoff of several thousand is *positive* and the stock *goes up*! What's wrong with this picture?

To show an example of this phenomenon, I'll share with you a 1994 *Wall Street Journal* article on the Xerox Corporation I cut out and saved. Now, this is not a criticism of Xerox, which incidentally I consider to be a wonderful company that may or may not survive, but it illustrates my point. The headline announces: "Xerox to cut 10,000 jobs, shut facilities, charges of $854 million are planned; net loss is likely for the full year." Approximately four paragraphs into the story it reads, "the magnitude of the new reductions caught some analysts by surprise; Xerox shares surged $5.625, or 7%, to close at $86.375 in composite trading on the New York Stock Exchange."

Do you know that Xerox shares have never jumped 7 percent in one day with the announcement of any new equipment, any new technical advancement, any new managerial change, any profit statement.... They announce that they are firing 10,000 people and the stock jumps 7 percent - great for the shareholders, but not necessarily for the 10,000 ex-employees.

Realizing that one of management's main jobs is to enhance shareholder value, then from the management and shareholder perspective, if it gets the stock up, let's fire a few thousand people – but let's not call it "firing"; let's come up with a more creative term that has a more positive spin. How about "downsizing" or "rightsizing"? If you can lay off 10,000 people and get the stock market to take a spike like that, why doesn't every big company lay off 10,000 people? Well, they have and they will again as long as the stock market's reaction is positive.

Another little known, but important aspect of reengineering is hidden in the glamour of the Bull Market that ran through the 1985-1999 time period. This ploy resulted in tax consequences for employee lay-offs, and the numbers are staggering. A major part of reengineering the company is to manage the layoffs and prevent a "riot in the street" in the community where the company is located as well as all the unpleasant publicity that could follow for the company; to do this the corporation would give bonuses to the "voluntary" downsized, kind of like throwing a dog a bone to keep it from barking. Now, when you lay off 10,000 people and you give them $40,000 retirement bonuses, where do you think the $400,000,000 comes from? You guessed it, the U.S. taxpayer. Through what is called NOL, a "net operating loss," a loss can carry back for three years or carry forward for up to fifteen years.

In other words, the company strategy was to create a loss of $400,000,000 through the layoff and then re-file the tax returns for the past three years and "get back" any taxes paid over the last three years and/or shelter profits forward. They sometimes made more money creating that loss than they did making and selling their products. Remember when the headlines read, "Changes of $854 million are planned, net losses likely for a full year"? *Likely*, my A_ _ (three letter word for derriere)!

There was a period of three years running where you couldn't pick up a business periodical that did not have a major article about reengineering, downsizing or rightsizing; it took me a while to put the puzzle pieces together. Our deficit in 1983, for the first time in America's history, was $1 trillion; by 1986 it was $2 trillion; 1989, $3 trillion; 1992, $4 trillion, and now is at a staggering 5.5 trillion dollars. One of the largest contributors to that amount has been the reengineering of corporate tax returns, coupled with the reduced withholding from employees.

Our political debates are all about taxing and spending, and the Democrats blame the deficit on the Republicans and the Republicans blame the Democrats and the Congress blames the President and the President blames Congress – actually we are ALL somewhat guilty: we want them to balance the budget, but not cut our favorite programs.

The main causes and effects of big businesses financials are rarely discussed because they are too complicated for a 30-second sound bite, and we live in a 30-second sound bite world. If you ask someone, "Don't you think G.E. should pay its fair share of taxes?" the 30-second answer is, "Well, if they had to pay more taxes, they'd just pass that on to us in higher costs for services. So we'd end up paying it one way or another." End of 30-second answer – when actually it is much more complicated than that.

The huge deficits came not from the political debate about changes in taxing and spending, but from big companies getting back all the taxes that they had paid through planned management created tax losses, and we were trying to fill up a bucket with no bottom. Every big company that had a major lay-off got back millions of dollars in taxes that they had paid or sheltered future profits – maybe someone ought to put a plug in the bucket so that there is no tax advantage to laying off 10,000 people.

Since 1985, hundreds of thousands of employees have been downsized, and their jobs are not coming back. In the 50s, 60s and 70s, when a big company laid off workers, especially key people, they couldn't wait to hire them back. Today, they not only won't hire them back, they can't wait to fire more if the stock results are positive. Now layoffs are so commonplace that they no longer have to give "golden parachute" bonuses to soften the blow or throw the doggie a bone to keep a worker quiet. They just lay him off.

The public corporate management mentality has changed from the employees and customers being the most important asset of the business to the stock value being the most important thing, and that drives a lot of management's decisions. I think that it is a shortsighted and a wrong-sided approach that will backfire - as "chainsaw" Al Dunlap found out. Add to that the major shifts in jobs and layoffs due to "robotics" and better computer technology in general, and thousands of additional jobs are eliminated. Machines do not require sick leave, health insurance or retirement programs. It used to be that whenever a company opened a $300,000,000 plant, 3,000-4,000 people were hired to run it. Nowadays, they have 60-100 people employed in the whole plant.

Another main business trend that we see affecting the world of work in America is globalization. You cannot stop a market-driven trend or the laws of economics; however, you must identify such factors and realize how they are influencing your environment.

A little over a year ago I was doing a two-day broker training program in the Sunbelt office in Rochester, New York. We were also doing a seminar on the advantages of buying an existing business or franchise at the Chamber of Commerce building because Xerox had recently announced a lay-off of 6,500 employees. Rochester is the "imaging capitol of the world," being the headquarters of Eastman Kodak, Xerox and the now bankrupt company formerly known as Polaroid. On the credenza in the Rochester Sunbelt office was a recent copy of the *Rochester Business Journal*. So I picked it up and took a look at an article that shocked me. It told the story of the cost of producing a sophisticated imaging system at Eastman Kodak called "The Professional." Now I have no idea what The Professional system is, perhaps a medical application or something, but here were the numbers. To produce The Professional in Rochester cost $55,300. Do you know how much it cost to produce The Professional in mainland China? A minor $1,400. Wow. Some difference!

Where do think that they are going to have to produce The Professional? You guessed it. The laws of economics are brutal. In the real world, Eastman Kodak cannot say, "By George, we are a great company and Rochester is a great company town, so we are going to keep jobs for our loyal employees here in Rochester and we will always produce The Professional here in the good ol' U.S.A." No matter how much they would like to be able to promise that, they can't, or the company could go broke. Kodak is forced to produce at the lowest price or someone else will. Thousands and thousands of jobs have been lost in the U.S. due to changes in the global market, and this was happening long before NAFTA.

There is another rather amazing shift in the world of economics and employment. That shift is in the country of Japan. Remember when we were growing up, the world seemed simpler in that "American made" products cost about this much; while products produced in Japan cost about half of that amount. Products produced in Taiwan or Korea cost even less. How things change. Japan is now a net importing country. Isn't that amazing? A few short years ago, one of America's largest economic problems was our trade imbalance with Japan, and that economy was so strong that the Japanese were buying up America. Now look what's happened to Japan's economy. Things have reversed. Where does Japan manufacture its automobiles? In the United States or in mainland China, where the labor costs are 1/10 what they are in Japan. Japan's economy is in serious jeopardy. The world of work and the world's model of job security has turned upside down on its head.

So, all in all, I believe that you are better off creating your own job security by going into business for yourself and running your business successfully. The family business has become the family farm; the family farm has become the family business. The jobs that are offered by a faceless company are somewhat less attractive. God has truly blessed America; we're big, we're strong, we're free and we're educated. We are the world's largest producer of goods and services and we are also the world's largest market for goods and services. I absolutely believe the old adage that as long as "America is good, America will be great," so long as God continues to bless us.

As I was completing this book, the unprovoked, senseless and cowardly act on the United States by terrorist thugs in New York City, Pennsylvania and Washington, D.C. has reinvigorated support for our government leadership and provoked a national unity not seen since World War II. We are a strong nation under God, and we will continue to get stronger.

Just how this "War on Terrorism" will unfold is uncertain, except as to its eventual outcome. We will prevail. Just how these events will affect the world of small business and the world of work is not clear except that in the short term, it has exacerbated the job loss of big companies as they adjust to new market conditions, real and perceived. I believe that many of these laid-off employees would be far better off going into business for themselves, rather than just seeking another job.

As the world changes, excluding the terrible tragedies of 9/11, I believe some of the changes are good for America's people. We're heading back to being a nation of shopkeepers and farmers, or in today's terms, small businessmen and businesswomen who are fiercely independent and who provide for their own job security and provide for their families by owning and managing their own business. They are building their financial portfolios by investing in themselves.

We are in the business of retail, service, manufacturing, distribution, restaurants, lounges, coin laundries, dry cleaners, liquor stores, multi-level marketing, franchise companies, professional consultancies - and independent businesses of all types. The structure of the business may be a sole proprietorship, a partnership or a corporation of some definition (such as a "C" corporation, an "S" corporation or a hybrid like an LLC, which combines some of the characteristics of the "C" and the "S").

But in essence, it's the small business or Mom & Pop business, as it is sometimes referred to, that provides the same necessities as a job does for you and your family. Providing an income for the owner, allowing him/her to provide for the needs of themselves and their families by paying the house and car payments and educating and feeding the children three times a day. Let's look back at my personal introduction to the family owned business.

Chapter 4

Growing Up

When I was growing up in Allendale, my dad was a small businessman in the community. He was a good, honest, hardworking, decent, smart and reasonably successful small-town businessman. Everyone in Allendale respected my father, many sought his advice, particularly in business matters, and there was never any question that Mr. Ben's word was his bond. He provided for my charming and sweet mother, my older brother Ben, my younger sister Lois and myself, and he gave us a good name. He was my hero.

Whether he was a farmer, banker, produce broker, tractor company dealer, motel owner, or restaurant owner - all of which he was at some stage of his adult life - he was successful, and he managed the business successfully. He never was a millionaire, but he was always successful. He was a wonderful father, and quite frankly, all I ever wanted was to be like him. Going through some of Dad's effects after he passed away in 1989, I found a note that he had kept since I was in the seventh grade. My teacher, Mrs. Margaret Boyelston, asked us one day to write a short paragraph in class about "our ambition." This is what I wrote:

My Ambition

My ambition is this...

I want to try for all I am worth to be as good a man as my father is. I want to try to live up to the good name he has made for his family and himself. I want to make something out of life as he does and is still doing. I want to help him in his business. This will be a very hard task, but if I work hard enough, maybe someday my dream and my "ambition" will come true.

- Ed Pendarvis 1956

Unbeknownst to me, the teacher had sent this note to my father and he kept it for the rest of his life. I haven't seemed to change much in the fifty years since then. I am still trying to live up to my dad and fulfill "My Ambition."

In Allendale, like other small towns, everyone either owned a small farm or small business or worked for someone who did. It was a great place to grow up. Business never strayed far from its traditional path, and even the elected officials discouraged any big business or plants from relocating to Allendale because it might take workers away from the small businesses and farms. Folks pretty much liked things the way they were.

Because U.S. Highway #301 went through Allendale and at that time it was the major North-South route from Maine to Florida, we had 13 motels in our little town. With a population of only 3,500, we had a Holiday Inn, Howard Johnson, and Quality Courts (which Dad owned), and many independents. Big farmers and motel/restaurant owners and bankers were the wealthiest folks in town.

In the late 1950s the federal government built the Savannah River Project, or "the bomb plant," as we in the counties of Allendale,

Barnwell and Aiken called it. It was the first "big company" to come to our area. The plant began hiring thousands of folks for higher wages than could be made at a small business or farm, and everyone wanted one of those government jobs. Things were beginning to change.

My first job, at age nine, was counting watermelons for Dad in the summer when the farm hands would load tractor trailer trucks or railroad cars full of watermelons to ship North to the market, where "the Yankees" paid a lot for fresh fruit. The third season, however, I was walking down to the produce shed one morning when Mr. Tom Keller, a prominent motel owner, asked me if I would like to be a bellhop at his motel every afternoon after school. He said he would pay me $1.00 per day, plus tips.

At the age of eleven, I resigned from farm work and headed for the bright lights, and better hours and cash, of the Allendale Motel. I've never looked back. In four years, I never missed a day of work except for the four days I was sick. Every afternoon from 3:00 to 8:00 p.m., seven days a week, I was there and made pretty good money for a kid my age, and I had no overhead. I was supposed to share a rotation of customers with the owner's son, Tommy, as they arrived at the motel. Tommy was older, had his own car and a girlfriend. She'd come over every afternoon and they'd sit out in the car and listen to the radio and talk. Consequently, I got to take most *all* the guests of the motel to their rooms. I learned two things that were pretty important: 1) be nice, polite and helpful to people and you'll get good tips; 2) don't let girl-friends get in the way of making money.

When I was fifteen, Dad bought the Quality Courts Motel, and I went to work for him and worked there through high school as a bellhop and later ran the office. I learned two things from that job: 1) you actually make more money as a bellhop than you do running the desk; and 2) you sometimes don't make as much money working for your family as you do working for someone else.

In 1961, after graduating from Allendale-Fairfax High School with a slightly better grade in football than in academics, I enrolled in The Citadel, the Military College of South Carolina. The first four years there were the most unpleasant; after that (since it was only a four-year school!), it wasn't so bad.

I went out for football my freshman year, but soon learned that although I had been a fairly good high school football player, I was too slow and too small to play college football. I'm not the brightest bear in the woods, but I do know that the avoidance of pain is normally the better track, and I quickly realized that professional football was not in my career plans. I made a decision to quit the team and try to find another path to enrich my life at The Citadel. Looking for any activity that would get me out of Friday afternoon parades and help me find an individual niche in a world where everyone wears the same uniform, eats the same food and shares the same schedule, I signed up to sell advertising for *The Sphinx*, The Citadel yearbook.

I liked selling ads. It was a lot less painful than football, and I believed in the value of folks supporting The Citadel. When I had reached my junior year, I had sold more ads than anyone ever had, so they made me Advertising Editor. I asked Col. McAllister, the Administrative Dean, who was one of the finest gentlemen I have ever met, to help me get permission from the Citadel to put together a staff of ad salesmen. As motivation for my sales team, I convinced Col. McAllister to authorize a short weekend leave (release) away from The Citadel each time a salesman sold at least $250 worth of advertising.

I learned two things: 1) if you get the right program going and the support of your superiors, you can accomplish a great deal; 2) if you offer a Citadel Cadet a weekend leave for $250 worth of advertising, you can sell $10,000 of advertising space in three months.

My academic record at college was, again, not outstanding, however, by the grace of God, I finally graduated with a gentleman's

"C" and some of the most beautiful "Ds" in Physics and Chemistry that you have ever seen.

I had some wonderful classmates in the Class of 1965. We formed an effective underground organization affectionately called "Fun, Inc." Every member of our class chipped in a few bucks and we rented a large beach house at Folly Beach, something that was absolutely against The Citadel's policy. We had a Board of Directors made up of one officer and one senior private from each of the seventeen companies at The Citadel. We also made a man across the street from the beach house, and the Police Chief of Folly Beach, honorary members of our class to keep them from calling Gen. Mark Clark, the President of The Citadel, or Col. Courvousie, "The Boo," to tell them about our escapade. As a final nod to the law, we hired off duty policemen to help direct traffic whenever we had a party. This organizational structure of one officer and one senior private was later turned into the official structure of the senior class Board of Directors which still function well at the Citadel.

With good friends supporting me, I was honored by being elected the President of the Class of 1965, and even though I seemed to be playing catch-up in my grades (I didn't graduate until August because of an unnamed physics professor), I was, for some mysterious reason, voted "Most Likely To Succeed" by my classmates. Go figure!

During our 30th reunion in 1995, the school was having the battle of its life; it seems that over $10 million was spent in legal fees trying to prevent women from entering The Citadel. Quite frankly, on that issue I probably differed from some of my Citadel buddies in that I spent four years trying to get a woman *into* the barracks. Everyone was now nervously saying, "The women are coming, the women are coming." Now, what's wrong with this picture? I've found that women do an excellent job in all professions, including the military.

Incidentally, a wonderful and successful author and storyteller, Pat

Conroy, has written several books about life at The Citadel and growing up in the South Carolina Low Country. He was two years behind me at The Citadel and graduated in the Class of '67. Pat has a great command of the English language and can paint a magnificent picture with words that are worth a thousand pictures. Many of his books have been made into films.

After The Citadel I spent two years on active duty in the U.S. Army field artillery. The Army sent me to the Republic of Korea rather than the Republic of Vietnam for thirteen months. It was a great tour of duty, and I learned a lot about the Korean people and their country. Then my duty rotation sent me to Fort Benning, Georgia, where I worked my way into Ranger School, which almost killed me! Great training, but if I ever go back into the mountains of North Georgia, it is going to be as a tourist.

Now it was time to enter the world of work. I had always wanted to go into business with my Dad; however, it just didn't work out that way. When I got out of the army in 1967, Dad wasn't very interested in expanding the motel business and the Eisenhower Interstate Project was building a highway called Interstate 95 stretching from Maine to Florida. It was rumored that it would take most, if not all, of the traffic off of Highway 301. We didn't believe that it would, but it did.

In Allendale, as in many South Carolina towns, the motel and restaurant business died a quick death after Interstate 95 opened. I learned two things: 1) a major change in a market trend can put you out of business no matter how smart you are or how hard you work; 2) you cannot stop or change a market trend.

In 1969, after working with Dad about a year, I decided that I had to move to Columbia, South Carolina, the state capitol, or Charleston, the capitol of charm and grace. I chose Charleston and I'm glad I did.

I called a bright, young, aggressive real estate developer and homebuilder that I had met in Charleston, Mr. Arthur Ravenel, Jr., and asked to meet with him about a possible job. Mr. Ravenel was kind enough to give me an interview, and I went there determined to get a job and learn the real estate and construction business from him. I offered to work for him for nothing for six months if he would teach me the business. Then at the end of six months, I would stay on with him, or not, depending on what he or I wanted at that time. At the end of six months he was kind enough to offer me a job at $1,000 per month working as the Vice President of the company.

We worked together well, and I learned a great deal from Mr. Ravenel. I also had the pleasure of marrying his oldest daughter, Suzie, in 1970. Suzie was and is a very fine and bright person; however, we had very different personalities and our marriage didn't last. She attended law school at the University of South Carolina, and after a few years we got a friendly divorce; we even used the same lawyer and threw a little divorce party together after the proceedings.

Here's another example, from my personal observation, of how the world of work has changed: when Suzie graduated from law school, there were four or five women in her class; when my oldest daughter, Stephanie, graduated from law school at the University of South Carolina in 1994, over half of the class was female. Stephanie is a very smart and talented attorney and she and the rest of her college classmates have turned out to be great lawyers, teachers, doctors, business executives and military officers or astronauts. Women also happen to be the fastest growing sector of small business owners in America – no glass ceilings here.

The growth and success of Sunbelt as a franchise would not be possible without the dedication, experience and valuable input from our female office owners and brokers. Some of our most outstanding franchisees are women. Debbie Moore in Reading, Pennsylvania, Pat Lawrence in Portland, Oregon, Joan Young in San Jose, California,

Karen Tipton in Tulsa, Oklahoma, Vienna Lee in Seattle, Washington, Laurel Johnson in Austin, Texas, Janie Abshire in Lafayette, Louisiana, Nancy Winters in Fairfax, Virginia, Suzanne Violet in Cocoa Beach, Florida, Myra Garrett in Asheville, North Carolina, Tricia Montoya, El Paso, Texas, and Laura Ujlaki in Ithaca, New York, are truly pioneers in our industry and integral to the success of Sunbelt.

I enjoyed working for Mr. Ravenel, later to be Congressman Ravenel and State Senator Ravenel, and one of the most effective public servants that I have ever known. One of his favorite sayings, "Nothing beats a failure, like a TRY," is a simple, but brutally accurate statement that has helped me persevere on many occasions when things just didn't seem to be working. However pleasurable as working for him was, in 1973, I had the opportunity to go into business for myself and I took it, never looking back.

In 1972 four men who were all millionaires (at least on paper), had started a 160-unit luxury condominium development at Snee Farm Country Club in Mt. Pleasant, South Carolina, a beautiful suburb of Charleston. They were about 50% complete with Phase I of the development of Ventura Villas (the first 32 units, swimming pool, tennis courts, land acquisition and site work) when the managing partner had a heart attack and died.

Each of the four men and their wives were personally signed on to a $4.5 million construction loan with a REIT (Real Estate Investment Trust) out of Silver Springs, Maryland. The interest rate was prime plus 5 percent, and the monthly payments of interest, at that time, were running over $20,000 per month. The monthly interest payments had to be paid or the REIT would not disperse the construction draw to the contractor.

Since the managing partner who died was the only one of the four owners who had been in the construction and real estate business, the remaining owners had both a major management problem and a major cash flow problem. They couldn't, or wouldn't, come up with the interest payments so the REIT had quit dispersing the construction draws and the contractor, MB Kahn Construction Company of Columbia, was threatening to shut down the job.

They needed $75,000 immediately to pay the back interest so that the REIT loan would be made current. They would then disperse the construction draw allowing the building to be completed. The owners were desperately trying to sell 25 percent of the project to anyone who had lots of money and real estate and/or development experience. They showed the project to every rich person in town who would listen to them.

At that time, there were only nine houses in the Snee Farm development (currently that number is around 1,000) and no one in Charleston could even spell condominium or figure out exactly what an "air lot" was (including me). However, I was invited to talk to the owners on behalf of my boss, Arthur Ravenel. Arthur had money and didn't want to lose it and said that he wouldn't touch the project with a ten-foot pole. He felt it had too many "hooks" in it and too many problems. They needed $75,000 right then, just to pay for the current and back interests payments.

There were two slight differences between me and everyone else who looked at the project: 1) they had a great deal of money, but didn't want the project; 2) I wanted the project, but (and it was a big BUT) I didn't have $75,000. I had about $3,000 in savings; I was a "little short" as we called that condition in Charleston.

I'll never forget that time in my life: I didn't sleep for three days, operating on sheer adrenaline. I kept looking at the project and running my numbers. There wasn't anyone in the world who was going to lend me $4.5 million to build a development, but the loan was already made.

I didn't need the entire $4.5 million, I just needed $75,000. So, where could I get $75,000? I went to see Dad.

Now my Dad was a smart businessman, and he was way too smart to lend me $75,000. However, because of my enthusiasm and the location, plus my four years experience in real estate and construction, Dad and a family friend (a big farmer in Allendale, Henry Wingo) agreed to lend me $75,000. All of a sudden I was a player.

Out of this experience, I learned three things: 1) finding someone who wants what you are selling is a lot more important than just dealing with folks who have a lot of money and don't want what you're selling; 2) don't ever try to qualify someone only by how much money they have - if they want something bad enough, they may find the money; 3) it's probably best not to buy something that's already killed one guy.

Well, we had some times. Mr. Ravenel was right; there were lots and lots of hooks, some with pretty sizable and very mean "barbs."

The first three problems that showed up was that the owners hadn't arranged for any permanent financing to "take out" the construction loans and, as I mentioned earlier, nobody in Charleston in 1973 could spell condominium, much less make a thirty year permanent loan on an "air lot."

The second problem we ran into was that we had some cost "over runs" that had to be paid for by the developers outside of the construction loans by the REIT. That bill was already over $110,000 and growing (the other owners had neglected to tell me about that).

The third unpleasantness was that when we all four "owners" had to come up with the next month's interest payments of $22,000 the "other" millionaires shared with me the fact that they didn't have any more money. To say that I wasn't having a very good day would be a little short of an understatement and I was beginning to get a clearer picture as to why the original partner "left."

Now, I don't want to give you the impression that everything in my life was going badly; in fact, it wasn't. The Lord has a strange way of leveling things out.

Over the years one of my favorite things in life that I've had the opportunity to participate in is the American Legion's Palmetto Boys' State Program. Through a series of lucky breaks and a dear brother and good friends who believed in me, I've had the chance to be very active in the Boys' State Program in South Carolina for thirty-nine years. I even had the opportunity to direct the programs for eleven of those years. It recharges your batteries each year to spend a week with 600 of the state's finest young men who are representatives to Boys' State from their respective high schools; however, by the end of this very fast paced week, everyone, including the Director is exhausted.

In 1974, after that year's exhilarating and exhausting week, I went down to visit Mom and Dad at our family's beach house at Lands End, a modest but comfortable place our family owned in Beaufort, South Carolina, across Port Royal Sound from Hilton Head Island. Mom and Dad spent most of the year down there now that Dad had "semi-retired."

Being somewhat of a confirmed bachelor and, of course, never having been around young children, I was surprised and shocked to walk in and see six kids running around the house, all under the age of four. At first, I was almost sorry that I had come down, even though my little sister Lois and my brother-in-law Tommy, both of whom I love dearly, were responsible for two of the six kids; six is a lot of kids.

Two of the children belonged to a couple who were close friends of Lois and Tommy, and the other two children belonged to a lady I had not met but found out later that I knew all of her family. Her name was Susanne Myrick, and she came from a small town - Estill - about 20 miles from Allendale. She had been married to a young man who'd been one year behind me at Allendale Fairfax High School and also at The Citadel. He had become a promising young lawyer, but was tragically killed in a helicopter crash a year earlier while on active duty with the Army National Guard.

I had not been at home when that tragedy happened but had read about it in the paper. Not knowing who she was though, I asked my sister, "Hey, who is that, she's cute." Without Susanne knowing it, my sister and brother-in-law had invited another young man down for the weekend, as a surprise guest and Susanne had not been happy about it. Fortunately for me, I looked good compared to him, who, because of the situation, she was a little mad at.

Out of the situation I learned three things: 1) you never know where the Lord will lead you (I had not even planned to go visit Mom and Dad that weekend); 2) sometimes you look better in comparison to others not because of your own attributes; 3) and if there are three people sitting on a front porch late at night and you get up to kiss your mom good night and excuse yourself to supposedly go to sleep and you quickly sneak out the back door, your mama'll go to sleep also and you can casually come around the outside of the house, and back to the front porch without looking too stupid. Anyhow, it worked for me.

Susanne and I started dating and sometime around ninety days later, I had a wife and two wonderful children: Stephanie and Elizabeth, who were at that time four and two, respectively.

Meanwhile, back to business.

It seemed as though several people were getting upset about not being paid, and I started having dreams about things like tap-dancing in a minefield. Telephone calls were not always happy occasions, and some folks began to think that I might not make it. The one thing that helped was that I was keeping in touch with everyone and working as hard as I could to get the project open; if we couldn't get Phase I open and start selling, we would be dead in the water.

We had set up two model homes for exhibits to show prospective buyers finished and furnished units, and Susanne, Stephanie, Elizabeth and I moved into a third unit that we used as a third model. I spent every waking hour and most of my sleeping hours trying to build, sell, close, finance or refinance the project.

Sometimes little, unexpected things help in a big way. Susanne and I took a "honeymoon" trip to Silver Springs, Maryland, to allow me to meet our REIT lenders for the first time and propose some restructuring of our loan arrangements. There was no way to pay the interest payments monthly and still have funds to get the project open. I desperately needed whatever money I could scrape together to do marketing brochures and get the road paved.

Well, during a somewhat tense part of my opening statement about the state of the project to the President and Vice President of the REIT, on the 12th floor of an office building in Silver Springs, Maryland, sitting at the largest boardroom table I had ever seen, a receptionist walked into the boardroom with some information the President had asked for. Of course, I stood up (a lady had entered the room!). Everyone else was a little taken aback.

The men and the lady were impressed with my manners, if not my lack of capital, and they agreed to a moratorium on interest payments until some date in the future. They also reluctantly agreed to lend me another $275,000 to start another building to show "movement" of the project. We now had some breathing room and some momentum.

Out of that experience I learned two things: 1) it is important to have good manners; 2) when you're dealing with a bank, it's far better if they already have millions of dollars invested in a project and you convince them that you are their best hope of getting it back.

While we had some challenging times (again, a little bit of an understatement), we continued to try to sell condominiums. Two other unexpected circumstances happened - out of a combination of hard work and pure dumb luck - that helped to save us.

With my marriage to Susanne in addition to a wonderful new family, I also got a riding lawnmower that I used to cut the grass at Ventura Villas. (Did I mention that I was the developer, builder, salesman, maintenance man, yard boy, painter and security guard?)

One Saturday morning as I was cutting the grass on the riding lawnmower, a blue Ford pulled into the condo area. I got off of the lawnmower, got into one of the two used golf carts I had purchased to make us look like a "resort" and rode over to pick up the potential buyers. I always showed everyone through the model homes personally.

As was the usual case, I showed this gentleman and his wife the two models and our home, which served as the third model. They were impressed with my family and our "hands on" involvement in the project. When they started to leave, the gentleman asked me if this was a project funded by an REIT out of Silver Springs and I said "Yes, sir." Well, it turned out he was Mr. Cary Winston, Chairman of the Board of the REIT in Silver Springs. He was kind enough to speak for me whenever they considered foreclosing on us from the standpoint that "we couldn't find anyone else who would work as hard as that fellow and his family at Ventura Villas to make the project successful." They had faith that through our persistence, perseverance, hard work, total commitment and luck that I would eventually pay them off. We had some trying times to say the least, but they never foreclosed, and they eventually did get their money back.

The other major problem at the time was that we could not get any local banks or savings and loans to give us any construction loans or thirty-year mortgages since these institutions all were convinced we were going to fail. However, the President, Vice President and Chief Loan Officers of First Federal Savings and Loan, the largest S&L in Charleston, were kind enough to agree to let me make a presentation to them about borrowing some money. The meeting lasted over one and a half hours while I presented my construction plan and business plan. They smiled, listened politely, asked a few questions and at the end of the meeting, the President, Mr. Howard Burkey, gave me a ballpoint pen with the First Federal logo printed on it and a "token" to get out of the parking lot. They still couldn't spell condominium.

Some more encouraging help and hope came from one of the first residents of Ventura Villas, a Mr. Bill Moore and his wife, Jackie, from Columbia, South Carolina. They had bought one of the villas for cash (he was a big time investor or something). One day he walked into my construction office and said, "Captain Ed," (he always called me that for some reason), "How much do you need to build one of these buildings?"

I said, "About $275,000."

He pulled out a cashier's check for $375,000 that he had just received on some deal and said, "Captain Ed, I'll lend you $275,000 for six months at 20 percent interest, discounted, to build a building, but you've got to pay me back promptly in six months or I will own it."

I thought about that for all of about three seconds and then said, "I'll tell you what; you let me put the entire amount in First Federal Savings and Loan in my name for the six months and draw down against it and I'll do it." It was a deal!

I put $275,000 in First Federal in my name, and all of a sudden the bank thought that I was doing great. The old adage that "a bank will gladly lend you money if you don't need it" comes to mind. The bank agreed to make some permanent, thirty-year "take out" loans and agreed to lend me $275,000 to construct another building of eight units.

All of a sudden we had two new buildings under construction and then Mr. Henry Heinsohn at State Savings and Loan agreed to lend me another $275,000 to start a third building.

As we got closer to the six-month deadline, I had four of the eight units under contract of sale and when the Cooper River Federal Savings and Loan agreed to refinance that building, I paid Bill Moore back within a week of his deadline. We started selling condos and built and sold the rest of the project somewhat successfully over the next several years. A major factor in my survival during that part of my life was my good friend and attorney, Bill Ackerman. His advice and guidance was invaluable.

Since we had used our condo as one of the model homes, my wife and children were constantly interrupted by me walking prospective buyers through our unit and introducing Susanne and the girls to them (they were my best "sales team").

In 1975, Susanne and I built a house on the lakes in Snee Farms and moved out of the condo for a little more family privacy. My three-and-a-half year old daughter Elizabeth, who was constantly busy filling in coloring books, was always annoyed by being interrupted in her coloring by me bringing customers through our villa. She would color *every* page, front and back completely, then start a new book. She has since grown up to become a wonderful teacher and artist. When she learned that we were moving out of the model into a house, she said, "Good, and nobody can come in." (Out of the mouths of babes!)

The greatest event of my life happened while we were living in that house: the birth of our daughter Sara in 1976. Now I had three wonderful daughters! Sara is truly a missionary woman and I do believe she is a very special gift from God. In addition, business seemed to be going pretty well, and our condo units were selling nicely.

In 1980, we bought and renovated a nice, but run-down and

abandoned house in downtown Charleston, on the historic tip of the peninsula, called "The Battery". Charleston is a beautiful, historical and wonderful old city and this proved to be an excellent real estate investment. We sold our house at Snee Farm for around $100,000 profit and paid cash for the house on The Battery, which we renovated using my construction company.

Basically, everything seemed to be going well; however, something called inflation and rising interest rates were about to become major problems for all businesses and the real estate industry in particular.

Also, in 1980 I was overly involved in community affairs and was serving as Chairman of the Board of Directors of the Department of Youth Services for South Carolina, a state agency that runs the juvenile justice system, including the juvenile jails. I was also Director of the American Legion Palmetto Boys' State Program (as I previously described), State Commander of the South Carolina American Legion, and Chairman of the Salvation Army Board for Charleston. I also became active in politics.

I had not been directly involved in party politics, so when I announced that I was going to run for an open State Senate seat, (Seat 2, of the five-member senate delegation) I was told by the Democratic County Party Chairman that I couldn't do that, that was the seat desired by, Paul Cantrell, presently an elected member of the House of Representatives. Not to be deterred, I filed for Seat 2 anyway, and even though I led the three-way primary race (much to my surprise), I was defeated in the run-off election two weeks later (not much to my surprise).

Business was becoming increasingly difficult as the cost of construction, like the cost of energy and the cost of money, began to break everybody, myself included. From 1980 to 1982, as interest rates hovered around 18.5 to 20 percent and inflation continued to rise, the old adage that there are two ways to get out of the construction and development business became clear to me: 1) "you either die" or 2) "you go broke." Well, I almost died and I went severely "South of broke."

Also in 1982, the same folks and political leaders who had beaten my brains out in the Senate race in 1980 were kind enough to ask me to serve as Charleston County Chairman of the Democratic Party. You see, when I decided to get actively involved in politics, I zigged when the rest of the South Carolina zagged – I became a Democrat when the rest of the South Carolina (and the world) became a Republican during the Reagan Revolution. That can best be explained when you consider that up until 1980, practically all of the members of the South Carolina State Senate and House of Representatives and the Governor and Constitutional officers were all Democrats. That also changed with the election of an admired friend, Dr. James B. Edwards, a wonderful man and respected leader as the first Republican governor in South Carolina in over 100 years.

The 160-unit development at Snee Farms was completed in 1982; however, I was taking approximately $10,000 to each closing to pay the short-fall, and the interest cost was running well over $100,000 per year. The banks were lending me money to pay the interest so that the loans would stay current, and I proved once again that you cannot "borrow" yourself out of debt.

Faced with impossible debts, I had to go through the humiliating experience of going to each of my bankers and explaining that I could no longer pay them. As you might expect, they were not very happy about that and so we made an agreement. I would not pay them back completely, and they would never lend me any more money. They have certainly kept up their end of the bargain. It took me 18 years to pay off almost all of my debts, except for the banks, and they don't seem to have suffered much.

This experience taught me two things: 1) don't borrow money if you don't have to; 2) when you do stop paying the banks, it doesn't matter at all that you have paid them on time and a lot of money over the past ten years – when you stop, you're the same as all the other deadbeats. Banks love to lend you money when you don't need it; when you need it, the banks are not to be found. They also have no qualms at all about seizing your assets, including your home, if you were foolish enough to put it up for collateral.

Fortunately, my wife and I purchased our home on The Battery in her name. We had paid cash for the house, and it had not been in any way security for my loans; if it had been, the banks would have taken my house and put my wife and children on the street in a heartbeat. A banker will cut your guts out and watch you bleed to death without batting an eye and then go to church on Sunday feeling good about themselves and even sing in the choir (not that I have anything against bankers, you understand).

I also tried to develop a real estate sales company franchise and even registered the name and trademark, American Real Estate Exchange (AmREX). The idea was to offer the advantage of a reduced commission to homeowners. However, I'll tell you that even though the real estate rules say the real estate board doesn't "set commissions" (that would be price-fixing), in 1982 if you even suggested anything other than the standard 6 percent commission, they treated you like a Democrat at a Country Club. Also, I did not have the capital to "stay the course." It seems I've always been ahead of my time or behind my time.

Upon completion of the development at Snee Farms, I was looking for a way to make a living and was determined not to continue in the construction business. As I had done so many times in my life, I "backed into" my next business or family farm - business brokerage.

A fellow that I had known for several years, who had owned a very successful restaurant and lounge in downtown Charleston, Mike Davis, had started a company called NL Business Brokers and he asked me to become a partner in the firm. Since I had no money, we worked out a "sweat equity" deal where I would come in as a partner and vice president of the company and contribute part of my commissions to the company for my half interest.

Just as I could not spell condominium in 1973, neither could I spell business broker in 1982; however, I took to this profession like a duck to water. When Mike had first told me about the business, I was not that interested because, as I told him, I didn't like financials, P&L's and tax returns. Numbers did not excite me that much. Mike told me that financials didn't have a great deal to do with it. He used to say, "Someone will not buy a business they do not like, no matter what the financials show, but they would possibly buy a business they like, no matter what the financials show." You know what? He was right. Buying a business is much more of an emotional decision than it is a business and numbers decision.

Just as you won't buy a house you don't like, you won't buy a car you don't like, you won't marry a woman or a man you don't like (although that may come about later); you surely won't buy a business you don't like. It takes a lot of energy to make a family farm or a family business work, and normally you won't do well in something you don't like – it will be tough enough even if you do like it.

During the two years that I worked with my partner, we had some terrific highs and lows. At one point we decided to reopen a restaurant and lounge in Charleston, similar to the one he had successfully run before, called the Harbor House. "You can never go home again" comes to mind, since the venture was a financial disaster. I ended up having to buy my partner out of the brokerage business for $1.00 and take on the assumption of tens of thousands of dollars in losses in both businesses and a severe shortage in our bank accounts. Had my brother Ben and sister Lois not helped me out with loans, I would have never made it. Out of this I learned two things: 1) when you think you have a problem with a partner, you probably do; 2) don't ever let someone else run your checkbook.

Also in 1984, I got involved again with a very tempting and expensive mistress that takes all your time and all your money - politics. In 1984, I ran for Congress from the first Congressional District of South Carolina as a Democrat in the most Republican election in South Carolina history. A very powerful and very popular President, Ronald Reagan, was running for reelection, as was South Carolina's most popular and wonderful senior senator, Strom Thurmond. I ran against a friend of mine who was a popular three terms Congressman, Tommy Hartnett.

I sold my business, NL Business Brokers, to make the race for Congress so that I could put all my efforts into trying to win. The only buyer that understood business brokerage in Charleston was my only (and larger) competitor in the city, a company called Sunbelt Business Brokers.

Despite my hard-fought campaign, the voters, in their wisdom, decided that I made a better business broker than a Congressman, and they voted overwhelmingly for me to return to the field of business brokerage. I received a mandate from the public to stay in business! So I went back to work with Sunbelt Business Brokers as a broker-agent, and over the span of three years, I bought out the ownership interest of the other three partners, one by one.

During this time of economic turmoil and overextended civic activity and politics that commanded all of my time, energy and money, something got shortchanged in my life - my marriage. I have always tried to be a good father, but I have not always been a very good husband, and my wife and I began drifting apart and living separate lives.

Susanne was a smart and excellent duplicate bridge player and spent many hours pursuing this interest; she did not like politics. When she was home, I was off politicking or performing some other civic activity or working and when I was home, she was off playing bridge. Our marriage did not survive this divergence of interests, and in 1982 we separated and were divorced in 1984. Fortunately, the Lord blessed our relationship even through the divorce and we have always remained good friends. When she was off at bridge tournaments, I would move back into the house and take care of our children, and when she came home, I'd move back into my apartment down the street. Incidentally, buying that nice home on The Battery is probably the best real estate investment I've ever made. It's a beautiful house with white columns and my ex-wife and husband-in-law still live there. Incidentally, Susanne and Mark McLaughlin are two of the top bridge players in the world and I am very proud of them.

I found solace and stability by focusing on business. I believe that helping folks sell or buy businesses is what the Lord sent me here to do. I like working with a seller, learning about him or her and their business and what's going on in their lives that makes them interested in selling. I call it their business story.

Most of the time, the reason for selling is human-driven – for instance, the owner may be retiring, in poor health, unfortunately, or the owner dies or is getting a divorce, relocating, wants to do something else or may just be "burnt out" or tired of the business. I like to think of it in the same way as moving from one perfectly good house to another. Not a thing wrong with that house, we just find somewhere else we want to live. Sometimes we change jobs or locations or sometimes we even change husbands or change wives - things just change as we go through life.

Out of that change comes a good business that is for sale.

Buyers, on the other hand, are normally looking for a way to provide for themselves and their families. Most folks are "buying themselves a job" when they buy a business. I also believe that the word entrepreneur is greatly overused in America today. Most folks in our market are not true entrepreneurs or risk-takers; they have been pushed into our market by circumstances. They are "forced entrepreneurs" who have been downsized, reengineered or right-sized or they have a job that they do not like, or one that they feel may not offer future job security.

When I first went into this business in 1982, there were only about three to five percent of folks who said, "I always wanted to be in business for myself." Owning your own business has been called the American Dream, but I am not so sure most folks think that. I think most people would still like a $70, $80, $90 or $100,000 per year job that they liked, felt appreciated in and had job security. Now I still feel that only three to five percent of folks out there have really always wanted to be in business for themselves; however, I believe that 50-60 percent now consider owning their own business as one of their best options, to provide for themselves, given the present world of work and lack of job security.

The government statistics are way off – as always, statistics can be used to show anything. The government says that unemployment is down (4-5 percent). What they don't count on is how many folks are *"underemployed,"* not unemployed. We are not talking about people here who are in the unemployment line. We are talking about people who are doing something to provide some sort of income. They are consultants, part-time employees, or free-lancers, just doing something to pay the bills while searching for work. There are very few high-paying jobs out there for laid-off executives, and there are very few jobs for folks over 40 – and who isn't over 40? And anyone over 40 is "eminently overqualified" for an entry-level job.

It used to be that when you sent out 10 resumes, you would get several job interviews and probably several job offers. Today, you send out 100 resumes and no one calls you back, especially if you are past the magic age. The main reason they won't give you the job is that they know you are not going to take a $30,000 per year position and stay there. You'll only take the job for immediate income and you'll be spending all your time trying to get a better job. Whereas a young person right out of school will consider a $30,000 per year job "great" when compared to their current salary of nothing. With a $30,000 salary, they can afford their own apartment and some wheels.

Job interviewers ask anyone north of 40, "Do you understand computers?" and we say, "Oh, sure. I can run Windows." The kid right out of college can write code, for goodness sakes; he can build computers! He's been raised on computers and video games. Who do you think the company is going to hire?

I'm in the same boat. No one is going to give me a $30,000 per year job because I cannot possibly live on that salary what with three daughters, and two stepdaughters, two ex-wives and two husbands in-laws. I am probably better off providing an income and job security by owning my own business. So are you!

Chapter 5
Finding the Right Business for You and for Me

When someone is looking for a job or a business to provide for him/herself and their family, I think the most important thing to do is to *find a business that you like*! I do not mean that if you like to go fishing you've got to get into the fishing business, but it's tough to put the necessary energy into something you don't like. If you hate to get up and go to work each day, then you've got a problem. I don't care how smart you are or what kind of business it is.

If folks are still having trouble deciding which direction to head, I like to ask them to think back to their childhood from ages 7-15. What did you like to spend your time doing when you were completely free to do whatever it was that you wanted to do? You used and developed your God-given talents in that period of your life as freely as you wished. You may now look at becoming the owner of your own business in the same way - and there are no limits to what you can do or what you can consider.

Another necessity for success in owning a business is a willingness to work smart, hard, long hours. You can forget the 8-hour day and the 40-hour week. Most of the folks I know that are successful in their own business put in 10 to 12 hours per day and 50 to 60 hour work weeks.

For instance, my brother Ben is a successful small businessman: he's a medical doctor, a pediatrician. Let's look at his and his wife Faye's investment in their success. Four years of college, four years of medical school, two years of an internship, two years of residency in his specialty, and then he began his service business. He worked at the hospital to pay his way through medical school and Faye worked as a teacher. He makes rounds at a hospital beginning at 7:00 a.m. and then goes to his office. He has some wonderful partners; however he is on call all night certain evenings and one weekend per month. He works hard and long hours and is successful.

I have heard that professional sports players usually work 30-hour practices for every hour in the game. That is after years of little league, high school sports and four years of college sports before they became a professional.

Fortunately, most folks who are successful like what they are doing and therefore the long, hard hours do not seem so long and hard.

In most things in life, as you climb the mountain of success, if you break the journey down into small steps, you will have a much better chance of success. I used to be in the construction business and learned something interesting. The international height of a step is 7½ inches. You can climb up several flights of stairs at one time, if it is a standard step. Have you ever tried to walk up steps that are a foot high? You'll get exhausted. It works the other way around also. Have you ever experienced a small step stairway, 3-4 inches? You almost trip because the human body is used to a 7½ inch step.

When making a decision, try to break the decision process down into small standard steps. Take life and business decisions one step, one day, at a time. When you look at a book on "How To Buy a Business in America," it usually tells you to first get the financials and take them to a good accountant. If it's a good business, he'll advise you to buy it. I've been in this business for almost 20 years and I've never once, *not once*, had an accountant advise a client to buy a business, unless it was a franchise. The accountants have been hired to protect their client, and if they are going to err, they are going to err on the side of caution.

Besides, accountants are only looking at the financials, not the business (the location, product or service, trained employees, furniture, fixtures and equipment, the existing customers, cash flow and the track record of the business). The financials have been prepared with one main focus, and that is to pay no taxes or to minimize taxes. They have not been done to show how well the business is doing. (More about how the financials relate to the value of the business, later.)

Secondly, the book on "How to Buy a Business" tells you to get these financials, do a great business plan and take them to your friend the banker with whom you play golf every Thursday, or know socially. Your banker has already assured you that he'll make you a business loan when you need it; after all, he is Vice President of (insert the name of your bank), the small business lender for your city. Yeah, right. He has already assured you that he'll lend you the money – *but he won't* – so don't operate under that impression and let that banker humiliate you on the golf course. Go ahead and beat him – bad. He's not going to lend you the money because he *can't* for reasons I will explain shortly.

Third, the book instructs you to go see a good business attorney. If it's a good business, he'll advise you to buy it; if not, he won't. Remember he has also been hired to protect you, not to do the deal – the only way to protect you totally is for you not to do the deal. If you do in fact do the deal, he will want to slant it so strongly to your side that the other side won't agree to the terms of the deal.

If you never want to take a chance that you'll have to go through the human pain and agony and heartbreak of a divorce, your attorney can protect you. Just don't get married, or get a prenuptial agreement to protect you. I don't know of a quicker way to kill a romance than to say, "Sweetheart, before we go any farther into this relationship, I want you to look over and sign this little agreement my attorney has proposed." Good luck! You won't have to worry about getting divorced because, unless you are Donald Trump, you'll never get married.

Don't get too upset with lawyers, accountants and bankers though – just realize that they have been trained to look for problems. They have been hired to protect you, not to help you do the deal and buy the business. However, when you don't buy a business you still don't have a job or an income so they have not helped you solve your problem. A business broker's job is to help you find a solution to your problem by helping you find the best business opportunity for you that will provide you an income.

The most important thing is to keep the focus on the business and to find a business that you like and feel you can manage. Normally you are much better off finding an existing business or a franchise than you are starting up a business, for several reasons. The existing business or a franchise has an established track record; the very fact that it has *survived* in the market place for three years or longer has a major impact on value.

Some special advantages of buying an existing business, according to my friend, Tom West, former President, Executive Director and Founder of the International Business Brokers Association (IBBA) and THE Acknowledged GURU of Business Brokerage are as follows:

An Existing Business Has:

1. Actual results, rather than a pro forma

2. Immediate cash flow

3. Trained employees in place

4. Established suppliers and credit

5. *Established customers and referral business*

6. *Existing licenses and permits*

7. *Training by the seller*

8. *The availability of owner financing; and this caveat: the success or failure of the business is the owner's responsibility and there is no "right" or perfect business, so buyers must be flexible.*

When I first bought the other folks out of Sunbelt, in the mid-1980s, we had an office in Charleston and one on Hilton Head Island. I learned really quickly that I could not successfully run an office that was two and a half hours away. This is a relationship building business, and relationships take time to build. Every time I would drive down to Hilton Head to meet with a buyer and/or seller, we would have a very good one or two hour meeting; however, nothing would come of it.

Also, every time I'd leave Charleston to drive to Hilton Head, I'd drive past 5,000 businesses and waste a day. I learned two things through owning the office in Hilton Head. 1) I re-proved the adage that I'd have a much better chance of helping a person who wants or needs a business than one who has lots of money and doesn't really want or need a business; 2) Hilton Head is a strange and beautiful place; everyone there is a multi-millionaire and you couldn't raise $10,000 *cash* on the whole damn island! I closed that office.

In 1986, again by happenstance or divine intervention, I met and fell in love with my present and *last* wife, Elaine. Our Sunbelt Business Brokers office was downtown on Church Street, near Market Street, and one day for lunch I went to the "food court" at Market Square. Out of the dozen small restaurants and their offerings, I decided to get a chicken sandwich at the Chicken Place. (I have always liked chicken.) In front of me in line was an attractive, cute, perky girl with the prettiest smile in the world. I overheard her order a hot dog (even though that was not the hot dog vendor) – the owner protested loudly, but then sold her what she wanted. I mentioned to her that this was a chicken shop; however, she had already prevailed.

After she left I asked Dorio, the owner of the Chicken Place, "Hey, who is that?" Dorio said she was named Elaine and that she had recently purchased a gift shop on Market Street. I, of course, asked discreetly and matter of factly if she was married and Dorio told me that she was recently divorced. I was off.

Upon walking into Elaine's Shop by accident (yeah, right), I ran into a little problem. It was primarily a children's gift shop, and I had trouble finding something that seemed appropriate for me to buy. I bought a little sand castle, which I still have, so that I could talk to her. Well, I couldn't think of much to say at the cash register, and there were several folks in line behind me so I made my purchase and left.

Being determined to make a good impression, I decided to buy a bottle of wine and drop it off with a note from Sunbelt Business Brokers saying "congratulations" on your purchase of the business. The only problem with that hastily put together plan was that when I went into the shop to drop off the wine, a man was in there, rather than Elaine. I asked him where Elaine was and he said she was out for a while. I took a chance and just left the wine and the note, wondering who he was. Fortunately for me, he was Elaine's brother, George, who is now my brother-in-law.

After several more minor purchases, some of which I was assisted with by my youngest daughter Sara, who was ten years old at the time, I finally got up the courage to slip Elaine a note in the check-out line. Basically it said that I could no longer afford to shop there; however, I would like to invite her to lunch or supper sometime.

She was surprised. Until then, she'd thought I wanted to list and sell her business, which nine years later, I actually did. After a few more slight miscommunications, we had our first date. I thought it would be a good idea to take her to my favorite seafood restaurant, RB's, on Shem Creek in Mt. Pleasant. It's a great place to sit on the water and watch the sunset.

She had heard that I was somewhat of a formal and "stuffed shirt" businessman who always wore a suit, so she dressed up. My kids, who tended to agree with the assessment that I was a "stuffed shirt" businessman, advised me to dress casual for the date. I purchased my first pair of khaki pants and tennis shoes specifically for the occasion. You can imagine how interesting our first date was!

Well, it was great - and being a persistent person, I asked Elaine out every night she could or would go after that. She had two daughters, Melany (14) and Jennifer (11). After approximately three months of my constantly hanging around, Elaine and I were having supper one night and she said, "Look, you're a wonderful man and I enjoy being with you; however, I have two children and a business to run and I simply cannot go out all of the time. I'm exhausted – we have to stop seeing each other so much and just slow down some."

Of course, I said, "No, that is not acceptable; that's not an option. Perhaps we should consider the… you know, the 'M' word." I've always been good at making quick decisions. Anyhow, I did ask her to please consider it. We agreed to have lunch on the following Friday and decide. At that lunch I said, "Well, do you want to get married or what?" and fortunately for me she said, "Yes."

Since we had both been married before, our church, Saint Philip's Episcopal, would not marry us, so we got married in the lobby of a beautiful old restored office building at 171 Church Street and got the Chaplain of the Salvation Army to officiate. Our five girls - my three daughters, Stephanie, Elizabeth and Sara; and Elaine's two, Melany and Jennifer - were our bridesmaids. We had a wonderful small family and friends wedding on November 8, 1986. Each of our girls are very special and unique and I have always been in awe of my children as they have grown up and developed as strong willed and discerning individuals. Melany has a masters degree in Art Education and Jennifer is still a work in progress. It will be interesting to see the book that our girls will write about their life stories.

Now, back to business. The year preceding our wedding, I had built our brokerage staff in Charleston to 14 agents. I determined that was too many, forcing me to spend all my time managing brokers when I like doing deals myself. So, I got down to just myself and one other broker, and that was too few. We could not possibly handle the volume of business and certainly could not dominate our market with only two brokers.

During that pared-down time in 1985, a very telling thing happened. I was attending a birthday party of a friend, Peggy Hendricks, and during the normal chit chat and pleasantries of seeing old friends socially, I ran into a young lady that I had known for years. She was a bright and charming daughter of a prominent businessman who owned the Budweiser Distributorship for lower South Carolina, Pearlstine Distributors. She had married a nice young man from California, who had soon learned one of the absolute "rules of nature": if you marry a girl from Charleston, you're going to end up having to move to Charleston. When I welcomed the groom to Charleston, his bride introduced me as Ed Pendarvis, owner of Sunbelt Business Brokers, and added, "*They're Huge!*" I'm thinking to myself, "*Huge?*" Just myself and the one other fellow and the one small office in Charleston? However, I found out she was on to something that has helped us grow.

Folks like the name "Sunbelt" and feel that they have heard of Sunbelt in a positive way. The "Sunbelt," a wonderful section of the country, a Sunbelt Coca Cola Distributor, a Sunbelt Construction Company, a Sunbelt Trucking Company, a Sunbelt Rentals Company, etc., etc. What's in a name? A great deal, thank you, and thanks to Susan Pearlstine for making me aware of that.

From 1986 to 1989 I tried different ways to grow. I bought a small corner grocery/convenience store with my brother-in-law, George, and he did very well there for a year or so. Then I made a mistake and pushed him to buy another store two blocks away. Again I proved to myself what I learned in Hilton Head: that you can run one business, but running two is not easy. After some frustrating times, we decided to sell the stores. George can fix anything, so he went into the construction business and I decided to stick with business brokerage. Fortunately, since we were business brokers, we were able to sell both stores for a profit.

Another time, I decided to buy a small manufacturing company called "Charleston Chimes" from a wonderful lady named Peggy Leland. She had developed a good product and a respected name in the local tourist market. Charleston has a thriving tourist industry with approximately 4 million visitors per year. The chimes were tuned to the Charleston church bells, and she made them in a small house behind her house on James Island with the help of a neighbor lady. She had built up a 20-store local customer base, including my wife's shop, Elaine's in the Market. At Sunbelt, many buyers were looking for a manufacturing company; however, they were looking for a much larger business, as Charleston Chimes was too small.

So, I bought the company, built a shed behind our home and went into the wind chime manufacturing and distributing business. We even took the product to the Atlanta Gift Mart for a couple of years. However, finding myself working until 2 or 3 a.m. making wind chimes, I proved again that there are only 24 hours in each day. I could not make wind chimes all night and broker business deals all day. I decided to sell the wind chime business before I cut one of my thumbs off cutting out the metal pieces.

Charleston has always been a wonderful artist's community and in 1992 I purchased the rights to all prints done by one of Charleston's favorite artists, Ed Emerson. I first met Mr. Emerson when I built him a condo at Snee Farms. He was a retired Navy Captain and he began his art career at our development. When he decided to retire, he came to Sunbelt to sell his line of prints. So, Elaine and I bought it.

I also started a small greeting card company called "Your House Greetings" through Elaine's shop. Folks could send me a picture of their house and I would draw a pen and ink sketch of it on a note card and run them off at Kinkos.

In the construction business, I used to draw up my own plans and I liked drawing houses. However, I could not draw enough of them to make a living, so I decided to stick with selling businesses.

In 1989, I sold a string of One Hour Martinizing dry cleaning plants and a "drop off" station to an accountant/businessman named Dennis D'Annunzio, who was moving to Charleston from Charlotte, North Carolina, with his family. He was and is a good, smart, experienced businessman, and he did adequate due diligence on his purchase. What he didn't realize; however, is how hot it gets in Charleston in the summer, and being from Detroit, originally, he found out the hard way that he hated the dry cleaning business.

He tells this story much better than I; however, he said he found out that if the "presser" or "spotter" doesn't show up, guess who's back there pressing and spotting in the 120-degree heat? The owner, CPA, President/CEO, or whoever else is in charge. Dennis says, "I'm not too worried about dying and going to Hell. I've already been there."

Since he hated the business, consequently he did not do well in it, and in 1991 he came back to Sunbelt. At Sunbelt we sell businesses to you and can sell them for you. We resold the dry cleaning businesses, and the folks that bought them are still doing well. One Hour

Martinizing is a good business; it just was not a good business for Dennis.

Dennis was looking for something else to do, and I suggested that he come and work with me at Sunbelt Business Brokers. It was the best business decision I've ever made. Fortunately for me, he agreed and he utilized his deal-making talents, unusual for a CPA, to be a very successful broker. Often times CPAs can only focus on the numbers; Dennis can focus on the people, the business, the product and the deal, as well.

A few months later, I invited him to breakfast at Nathan's Deli and suggested that he come into Sunbelt Business Brokers as an equity partner with me. I thought that we could grow the company together, because the need for this type of business service was so great. I told him that I felt that we had something to sell and that if he would join me, neither of us could take a salary initially, because the company could not afford it. We would have to live on our personal commissions; however, if he joined me, I'd make him a millionaire.

Dennis is a smart, hardworking, determined businessman and a friend, and we complement each other. In 2000, at Sunbelt's annual meeting in Charleston, I asked him to serve as CEO of Sunbelt, handling all operations for the company as we continued our growth. This past year I asked him to serve as President and CEO. Also around this time, we were fortunate to add another powerhouse broker to our Charleston offices. Tom Conroy, as President of the Charleston Sunbelt Office. This allowed Dennis and me to focus our efforts to growing the Sunbelt franchise.

In June of 1991, we opened an office in Greenville, South Carolina, and within 90 days of opening, we had the best, and largest business brokerage firm in Greenville, even though there were five other existing business brokers in Greenville when we started.

We did the same thing in Columbia, South Carolina; Charlotte, North Carolina; Augusta and Savannah, Georgia; and Myrtle Beach, South Carolina. In 1993, we filed our franchise documents. We got our Federal Trademark Registration and began franchising in earnest. The Lord has truly blessed us, we have been growing at a steady 30 percent per year and now have over 300 offices in 45 states and 11 foreign countries.

At Sunbelt we've been fortunate enough to attract some wonderful and bright franchisees (partners) and associates to help us develop our market presence. I have learned a great deal from each of our franchisees, especially Tim Rogers in Sacramento, California, Dan Elliot in Houston, Texas, Ron Hottes in Los Angeles, Carl Grimes in Fayetteville, Arkansas, Scott Evert in Minneapolis, Minnesota, Bill Law in Charlotte, North Carolina, Doug Jackson in Washington D.C., Deb Moore in Reading, Pennsylvania, Dan Pedersen in Kansas City, Missouri, Pat Lawrence in Portland, Oregon, Ray Boreham in Atlanta, Georgia, Franco Ferrari in Orlando, Florida, Jeff Moody in Dothan, Alabama, Steve Stone in Virginia Beach, Virginia, Sonny Adams in Memphis, Tennessee, Roger Hutson and Matt Ashburn in Des Moines, Iowa, Herbert Lonegrass in New Orleans, Louisiana, Steve Rosen in Philadelphia, Satish Patel in Boston, Steve Goldberg and Jack Armstrong in New Jersey, Len Krick in Las Vegas, Greg Kells in Ottawa, Canada, and Greg Lange in Thailand.

In the January 1995 issue of *Entrepreneur* magazine, Sunbelt was rated the number one business brokerage franchise in America in their annual listing of the Top 500 franchises. We repeated that designation for '96, '97, '98, '99, 2000 and 2003 issues. We made the top 100 fastest growing franchises, normally sustaining our growth at a rate of 30% per year.

In 1995, Sunbelt had 35 offices, by 1996 we had 65, by 1997, we had 97, by 1998 we had 132, and by 1999 we had 178; and by the year 2000 we had 218 offices in 40 states and 8 foreign countries.

When Dennis and I first put together our franchise program, we did two things considerably different from other franchisors. First we decided to have a "flat fee" franchise fee, rather than a percentage or royalty that would have been based on a percentage of gross sales of our franchises. The idea being that when someone became very successful, they would have the incentive to *stay* with Sunbelt Business Brokers, not *drop out* because the percentage royalty became too much money as they became more successful. Second, we decided that to help our offices be successful, we had to put a great deal of emphasis on training and train not just the office owners, but all the individual brokers as well. I am President of the company, now Chairman, but I have personally trained every broker and agent, one on one, over the last ten years. That has proven to be a good idea and has afforded me the wonderful chance to meet every broker in every office.

My friend Bill Law in Charlotte, North Carolina, our fourth Sunbelt office, has been very successful, normally doing well over $1,000,000 per year in commission income. If Bill had to send us $60,000 or $80,000 in royalty payments, he probably would have dropped out of the Sunbelt Network long ago. His fee is constant and is an incentive to stay with Sunbelt rather than drop out. I haven't trained a broker in Charlotte in over four years. He has a stable and professional group of eight brokers who have been with him for years. However, we probably trained over 30 brokers in Charlotte before he settled on the core professional group he has.

Bill is an important fixture on the Sunbelt Team who has been good for us, and we applaud his success. We also decided that we would have to train all the brokers/agents because business brokerage is a very different and difficult business discipline and very few folks know how to do it. So we set up a training program where we hold a two-day "basic business broker training class" every week. We started our training in Columbia, South Carolina, once a month for offices in Columbia, Greenville, Spartanburg, Myrtle Beach, Charleston, Charlotte, Augusta and Savannah. As our office network grew, we moved training to Charlotte, Atlanta and Orlando every month. Then to Washington D.C., then L.A., Dallas, etc.

Sunbelt Business Brokers also had no national advertising fee since we believe the local office knows best how to spend the precious advertising dollars in their market. We recommend $250 to $500 per month in the yellow pages and $1,500 per month in the largest local Sunday newspaper. We advertise in the "Business Opportunity" or "Business For Sale" section. Also, realizing that business brokerage was such a different field from what anyone had done before, we decided to invite *prospective* brokers and franchisees to our training without cost or obligation.

At first, everyone we talked to said that was not a good idea; however, we felt that since this was such a different business from what people think and know, we'd rather spend two days with someone – get to know them a little bit and get them to know us and the Sunbelt System before we sign an agreement and become partners. A franchise is a partnership by definition whereby we license someone the use of the Sunbelt name and the Sunbelt system of business brokerage that we feel works. Out of our mutual success they pay us a flat amount every six months as a fixed royalty. This royalty never goes up. This concept has allowed us to build a strong platform of impressive franchise partners who have led Sunbelt to success worldwide. Many of our franchisees make a lot of money.

This business attracts executive-type, independent, self-confident people, and we've got some real superstars. (More about them later.) It is also a testament to our franchise operation that we have never once had a lawsuit with one of our franchisees.

We felt, and still feel, that the main obligation of training is to get a broker to understand and believe in the value of small business. His or her success depends on their understanding of the small business, and understanding the sellers and the buyers, and also understanding a proven system of how to help them get to where they want to go. I call it the buyer's and seller's *Goal Line*. I also figure that I've got about 90 days to help a new broker make some money as a broker, or his wife will make him get a "real job." So I try to get a new broker up and running as quickly as possible.

Doing all of the initial training for Sunbelt has proven very helpful to me because, through training, I know personally who is on the other end of the telephone and so do the brokers I've trained. Those two days together help us build a relationship. Relationships are everything in this business, as in life in general, and we at least have had the opportunity to share ideas about the basic approaches to this business and strategies that help our brokers to better serve our clients and customers.

In a real estate deal, there is no "real" relationship between the seller and the buyer; in fact, most folks don't even know who owned the house they live in now, before they bought it, or whom they sold their last house to. Most often the buyer and seller don't even meet each other until what I call a one-hour "happy talk" meeting at closing. Normally the closing in a real estate deal is the beginning and the end of a brief relationship between the seller and the buyer. It's the Alpha and the Omega of the relationship and transaction. What a different world from business brokerage!

In a business deal the closing is the *beginning* of the relationship - especially if the seller finances a part of the sale price for 5, 7, or 10 years. Since the seller is going to finance at least part of the sale, a substantial portion of his money is invested in the continual success of the business *after the sale*. The closing *begins* the relationship between the seller and buyer. If you buy a franchise, the closing *begins* the relationship between the franchisor and the franchisee. Remember that in business, relationships are everything. It is the relationship, both personal and financial, that makes the deals work. The main focus of our business has always been on listing businesses to sell when an owner wants or needs to sell and helping a buyer find a business to buy when he wants or needs to buy; working with both parties to arrive at a price and terms and conditions that work for all parties; a level playing field; a win-win relationship.

Business brokerage is different from any business that I have ever been in. You have to build an honest relationship between the seller and the broker, between the buyer and the broker and between the seller and the buyer. Unlike real estate, where you normally have a broker dealing with the seller and another broker dealing with the buyer, in most business sales, the Sunbelt broker is the only broker involved in the transaction. I like that for two reasons: #1 we have to be sensitive and responsive to both the buyer and the seller, and #2 there are very few commission splits, so we get a $1.00 dollar, not a .50 cents dollar. However, let's look at the real value a business broker brings to the marketplace.

Chapter 6
The Real Purpose and Value of a Business

What's the real purpose of a business? Some folks would say the purpose of a business is to make a profit. Some would say the purpose of a business is to get and keep customers for your product and/or service and others would say it's to be a viable economic force that provides a product and/or service. I think the real purpose of a business is to provide a living or an income for the owner and his or her family.

What do you want or need out of a job? I assume it is the same thing, to provide a living or an income for you and your family. Now, hopefully the business or job will also be rewarding in other ways: challenging, interesting, growth opportunities, etc; however, one thing it must offer is financial reward sufficient to make you a living.

So ultimately, the question is, do I take this job? Do I start this business? Do I buy this business? You can work for someone else or you can work for yourself. What you need from that job or that business is enough money or earnings to provide for yourself. If I take this job; if I "buy" this job; if I buy this business, how much money will I make and will I have the opportunity to grow from there; income and otherwise? Well, to get the answer to these very important questions, we have to define our territories, borders or boundaries, so that we are on the same sheet of music.

Let's look at the world of business as seen today in America. Everything we study in school about business, every subject we take in formal education in America, especially in college and post-graduate study is about *big business*, publicly traded companies and giant private companies. All we see and hear from the talking heads on TV is about big business. Everything we read in the newspaper is about big business news.

What happened today on the New York Stock Exchange? What happened on the Nasdaq? What happened in the Standard and Poors Index, etc? When you realize that all we study in school and see in the media is about big business, this explains our understanding and interpretation of business rules and definitions, all pertaining to big business (mostly publicly traded companies).

No one graduates from college, gets a diploma and knows one thing about running a convenience store, dry cleaning plant, auto repair business or restaurant. They know a lot about running IBM, General Motors, Coca Cola or Microsoft, but very little about the real world of small business.

Isn't that strange when you realize that approximately 98 percent of businesses in America are small businesses. Our entire educational plant in America is geared toward one thing – get a job, and work for someone else in big business.

The Small Business Administration (SBA), our government, defines a small business as one that generates less than $20,000,000 in gross sales per year or has 100 employees or less. Isn't that weird? In the "real world" of small business that's a *huge* business. The government doesn't even know that we exist and that is probably good, not bad. They even quit trying to keep records and statistics on small business in 1996.

You have to understand that everything is relative. The government calls General Motors, Exxon, Wal-Mart, AOL and Microsoft big business. A medium sized business would be one that generates from $100,000,000 to $500,000,000 in annual gross sales. Under $100,000,000 down to $20,000,000 is a smaller sized business and under $20,000,000 is a small, small business.

Of all businesses in America, 95 percent do $1,000,000 in annual gross sales or less and have 20 employees or less. Another 3 percent do $30,000,000 or less and have 100 employees or less. The government and our colleges and universities do not know that small business exists and yet small, small business have provided all the jobs and family incomes that big business have been shedding for the last twelve years.

Here is an example: let's say that I own a convenience store along the road on the way home in any big or small city. One fellow stops in to pay for his gas and some convenience items and he says, "Ed, can you believe what happened in the stock market today? The Dow dropped 282 points!" I say, "Wow! Isn't that unbelievable? That will be $28.17, Mr. Jones." The next person in line says, "Did you see what happened today in Russia (Afghanistan, China, India, South America…)?" I say, "I'll tell you, Mr. Johnson, you never know. It's always something, isn't it? That will be $17.23." The next lady says, "Ed, can you believe what the school board, the Federal Reserve Board or the President, or the Democrats are doing? It's terrible." I say, "Yes, ma'am, its always something. That will be $19.88." Etc., etc., etc.

At the end of the day; at the end of the week; at the end of the month – no matter what happens in the world otherwise, I have made enough money to pay all of my business expenses, also my house payment, my car payment and I have fed my children.

Small business, sometimes referred to as "Mom & Pop" businesses, is America's Amazing Economic Engine, and it runs right along through the ups and downs of the stock market. It runs right along through the ups and downs of interest rates. It runs no matter who the president is or what Congress does and no matter what's happening in China, the Middle East or on the world stage otherwise. Small business is the stabilizing force that does exactly what it is supposed to do, which is to provide a living for the owner and his or her family and it provides all the jobs that the big companies have eliminated. It is the real economy. It is indeed America's Amazing Economic Engine!

Now small business differs from big business in some major ways, so for the purposes of getting on the same wave length, please let me share with you some of the things I share with all of my business brokers in training.

You see, when I do the new broker training sessions for Sunbelt Business Brokers, I feel that the most important part of training is to help our brokers see the real value of a small business. Because they are just like the rest of us, they have come out of a background and educational plant that only understands and promotes big business.

Three major differences in big business and small business as they relate to the real world are found in the areas of #1 financials; #2 management; and #3 what I call the size of the commitment. Also it helps to realize that what we call big businesses are normally "publicly traded" companies. Stock market companies that sell shares of stock or equity in the corporation to the public as well as to large investors, such as banks, college investment groups, retirement programs, union benefits, insurance companies, mutual funds, other corporations, etc. They may have thousands or even millions of "owners" or stockholders.

Big businesses have "audited" financial statements, and they have to comply with GAAP or Generally Accepted Accounting Practices, as set by accounting regulations. The financials have to be current, correct, complete and audited by an unbiased CPA firm (unbiased except that they would like to keep the company's business, of course, as in Arthur Andersen and the Enron Corporation scandal).

First, let's look at the financials. Have you ever heard the axiom that a business has two sets of books? One set for management purposes and another set of books for the IRS? Well, it's absolutely true! *Big business* has two sets of books while small business usually only has one set of books that aren't too accurate, current, or complete. In big business, one set of books is for public consumption with a nice glossy print prospectus that is sent to you when you purchase stocks. For instance, when you buy stocks in General Motors, IBM, Coca Cola, Microsoft or McDonald's, they send you a nice overview of the company with re-cast financial statements complete with notes to the balance sheets and income statements and a nice optimistic report from the president of the company or the chairman of the board. Great prospectus!

Now let me ask you something. Have you ever seen the tax return for General Motors? For IBM, Coca Cola or McDonald's? Absolutely not and you never will. That information is compiled on the other side of the accounting house with all the smart CPAs and tax lawyers doing everything they possibly can to "legally" take advantage of the tax laws and tax codes to help their clients pay no taxes or the minimum amount of taxes.

You would not believe how much money General Motors "loses" for tax purposes. General Electric from 1981-1984 not only paid no taxes on over $6.2 billion in pre-tax profits, but they got back $273,000,000 they had already paid in taxes (remember the net operating loss scenario). There is nothing legally wrong with this practice no matter how wrong it seems. The big business companies take advantage of all of the tax laws that their lobbyists have gotten Congress to write to protect the "cash flow" of the company, to build and grow the company and to enhance shareholder value.

Small business doesn't have the luxury of having two sets of books. They do not need and cannot afford a glossy print prospectus for public stockholders; they are a "private business" and no one sees their books. So they only have one set of books and they are normally not very accurate, complete or current. However, just like the big companies' second set of books that the public doesn't see, the books of a small business are done to take advantage of the tax laws and tax codes to help their companies pay no taxes or at least minimize taxes.

Small business owners also attempt to protect the "cash flow" of the company to provide for the needs of the business, to grow the business, and to enhance shareholder (owner) value. They teach you in school that the purpose of the business is to make a profit, right? No, profit is a bad word when it comes to taxes. You have to pay taxes on profits.

Your business can do $300,000 in annual gross sales or $3,000,000 in gross sales or $30,000,000 in gross sales; if at the end of the year the business shows no profits for tax purposes, no taxes are due. In fact, if a business shows a loss for tax purposes, you may use that to shelter future profits or perhaps get back taxes you paid the last three years on prior profits. When a big company announces a lay off of thousands of workers, a restructuring charge is taken, and they write it off.

Now please understand this is a very important part of the real world of business, especially small business. You can go for *years* without a profit, but you cannot go a *week* without cash flow. A business will not survive for long without cash flow or earnings even though for tax purposes it tries not to ever show a profit.

A second area of differentiation between a big business and a small business is in the *management*. The president of General Motors, for instance, sits in his corner office on the 22nd floor of the General Motors office building, which I assume is in Detroit. Well, he has to have correct, accurate, complete and current financial data to help him manage the company. He could not possibly walk through every manufacturing facility, every sales office or showroom, every financial department, parts department and service facility, much less the R&D Department and keep up with the leasing programs and advertising programs without current, accurate, complete and correct financial data.

The small business owner (Mom & Pop) opens the store (restaurant, dry cleaners, auto repair, etc.) at 7:00 a.m., and they are there working in the business, dealing with employees, customers, vendors, equipment, inventory, stocking, production and sales all day long. They do not use financial data to run their business because they are too busy "running" the business.

In fact, after running the business from 7:00 a.m. to 7:00 p.m., the last thing in the world they want to do is stay there another hour and make sure that the books balance. Mom & Pop need to go home and take care of themselves and the kids because they have to be back at the store again tomorrow morning at 7:00 a.m.

Small business owners don't use financial data to manage their business; they manage it by being there, and they normally use what I call "checkbook accounting." They know how much money they have in the bank; they know what the payroll is on Friday; they know the approximate amount of accounts receivable and accounts payable; they know the normal level of inventory; they know when the rent is due; and they know how much business they did last March, last April and last May. Their operating "books" are primarily their checkbook.

Mom & Pop use their total knowledge of the business to manage their business, and the accounting function (the books) are almost always in a catch-up mode. Sometimes I'll ask a small business owner for their books and records for this year and they'll say they are working on them. Heck, they don't even have last year's books yet, because they still owe their accountant for 1999. Accountants sometimes have to live with twelve-month receivables; however, they know you have to come back to file next year's taxes. They will eventually get paid, God bless them. And when the small business owners do finally get the financials to their accountant, they are usually only interested in one thing: do we have to pay any taxes? Then the annual financials go into a folder, never to be seen again unless or until the owners go to sell the business.

Folks in California think that they are the ones who come up with all these new sayings and expressions. They believe they came up with the phrase "walking around management." Shoot, Mom and Pop have been using "walking around management" ever since they have been in business. It obviously works.

The third area of differentiation between big business and small business is found in what I call the "Size of the Commitment in Investment." When you buy stock in a big business, you normally do that with extra money or savings that you do not use for living expenses. This money is after the basic expenses of house payments, car payments, education and eating three times a day. That money could be spent, put in savings or invested in stocks or bonds. There is no doubt that the discipline to put away that extra money in investment is important.

However, compare the size of that decision to putting practically all of your life savings into the down payment on a business purchase or start-up and add to that the additional commitment of having to get up every morning for the rest of your known life, at least six days per week and going to work there for eight, ten, twelve hours per day.

Look at the difference in the size of the commitment. One is a somewhat passive investment that could be stopped if you chose to, and the other is virtually a total commitment by you and your family.

Also, there is one other major difference between big business and small business that must be understood to arrive at the real value of small business. There was a period from about 1996 to 2000 when everyone seemed to get stock market fever. The normal returns on investment of making 5-6 percent per year in a bank savings account secured by the FDIC, and perhaps doubling that in the risk of the equity or stock market, gave way to exuberance in the stock market as folks begin making at least 20 percent return and up in stocks.

Some new IPOs or Initial Public Offerings on new technology companies that no one had ever heard of became overnight successes. Stock prices shot up hundreds of percentage points, even though these companies didn't have a product or service defined by the real world market, yet. The "old rules" of the economy just didn't apply, said some.

Folks signed on to these companies as investors bid up the stocks and many made fortunes. (*If* you sold the stock at the right time.) Folks quit worrying about their jobs and became "day traders" and stock market "gurus." Investment groups sprung up in neighborhoods.

The day traders, the stock brokers and the employees with stock options, the dreamers and the computer geeks that stayed up all night eating pizza and doing "cool" things on their computers, as well as a lot of very successful Wall Street investors, were riding high and kind of laughing at the rest of the world that missed the ride up. Guess what they found out? Old rules *do* apply. A business, big or small, has to make money. It has to have sales, not just "eyeballs" looking at a Web site that does cool things, and it has to take in more money than it costs to run the business or the business will go out of business. It will not survive.

Now, there is "blood all over the floor" in Silicon Valley and in many technology companies and in some areas of the stock market.

The day traders are all looking for day jobs. Stock options in many areas were not a good option, and the old rules of investment are back. Good, solid, well-run companies that make a product and/or service that the market responds to and that have earnings are a good long-term investment. How does that relate to the value of a small business? Let's take a look.

For a business to be successful it must have a product and/or service that the market responds to by buying that product or service. Sales drives value, and the old and new business rules say that for a company to be successful it must have more sales, revenue or income than it has in the total cost of production and delivery of those products and/or services. In a small business there is normally only one source of income, the sales of the business's product and/or services.

Now in a stock market company or a publicly traded company there are two major sources of income: 1) the sales of the company's product and/or service; 2) the sale of the company's stock or equity. So their business model is different from a private company, and it is a huge difference.

One of the main advantages of "going public" is the sale of the company's stock, in addition to the sale of its product or service that can raise tons of "new" money to help a company grow. However, at some point, the old rules that the company has to take in more revenue in sales than it costs to produce those sales comes into play, or they start burning right through the money that they received from the sale of their stock.

In the last six months of 1999 and into the year of 2000 the operative word on Wall Street was the *"burn rate."* How fast will this or that company "burn" through this IPO cash before it makes more on the sale of its product or service than it costs to operate or it crashes and burns. And the burn rate can go backwards, too. All through the food chain of investors, big and small, we learned once again that the stock market could go down, as well as go up. For some companies, however, where the marketplace did not respond to its product or service, it was and is not coming back up.

Webvan is a great example. The online grocery home delivery announced it was ceasing operations, laying off its last employees and closing up shop after burning through $835,000,000. Wow! One thing a lot of technology companies forgot is that Americans like to shop – we don't hate to shop. There are a lot of products that we go to the store to buy, and remember the retailer brought the stores and their products to our neighborhoods.

Again, compare that to small business: a restaurant, dry cleaners, auto repair, or retail business, whose "burn rate" is immediate. They do not have the luxury of tons of investment money through stock sale or investor money. They have to take in more money every week, every month and every year than it cost them to operate their business or they will go out of business.

Therefore, the very fact that they have been in business for three years, seven years, twelve years or longer, tells me beyond a shadow of a doubt that they are taking in more money than it cost them to operate their business; otherwise they would have never survived. They not only took in more money than it cost to operate the business, they took in enough extra money so that they could also pay their house payment, their car payments, feed and educate their children and perhaps even take a vacation – maybe even invest in savings or the stock market (hopefully not Webvan).

The one thing I know for sure is that if the small business were not paying the owner's bills, he or she would go out of business. The laws of economics are brutal, disregarding how smart you are, where you went to college, what your race, creed, national origin or who your daddy was. And the laws of economics always apply.

Let's use a sports analogy to help define the difference between big business rules and small business rules and real estate rules. I call big business rules "football rules" and small business rules "baseball rules" and real estate rules "basketball rules." Now, all three are ball games, each has a team of players and play in an arena; however, it sure is a different set of rules for each ballgame.

If you tried to play a baseball game in a basketball arena, every time someone hit the ball it would go up in the stands – homerun! Everyone would be a Mark McGuire or a Sammy Sosa. In fact the game would get boring after the score got up to 176 to 157 or so.

And if you tried to dribble a basketball on a football field or on a baseball field, it would obviously not work. You see what I mean - you simply have to use the right set of rules for the right ball game.

Most buyers, particularly if they are well-educated college graduates or have a post-graduate degree or have had work experience in big business, know chapter and verse about big business rules (football rules) and real estate rules (basketball rules), but they do not know anything about small business rules (baseball rules).

Often someone comes into my office who has got a wonderful and extensive business background, was Vice President of this or that "Fortune 500" company, has a resume that will knock your socks off, a master's degree in business. Well, he knows a great deal about football rules, but he doesn't know beans about small business rules (baseball rules). The problem is he doesn't know that he doesn't know, and so I really have to take some time and educate him about baseball rules.

Now if someone comes into my office who has *two* Masters degrees, that means he knows "twice as much about nothing." I usually have to put on an extra pot of coffee for this guy because it is going to take awhile to reeducate him about baseball rules.

So for purposes of our discussions about business and business value from now on we will not use real large businesses or publicly traded businesses. For our purposes, we will describe *small business* as those doing $1,000,000 in gross sales annually (or less) and that have 20 employees (or less). We will describe *big business* as those doing $1,000,000 to $30,000,000 in gross sales per year, privately held, and that have 100 employees (or less). We'll use baseball rules.

Chapter 7
Business Brokerage Is Not Real Estate Brokerage

We saw how football rules differ from baseball rules; now let's look at how baseball rules (small business) differ from basketball rules (real estate). Often times, folks will assume that since business brokers list and sell other people's assets or property, they are just like real estate brokers. Well, as the Hertz Car Rental ad says, "not exactly." The two professions differ greatly in application. Yes, the business broker lists and sells things; however, the similarity of the two professions pretty much ends right there.

Baseball rules differ from basketball rules in seven major ways:

1. Confidentiality
2. Financing
3. Relationships
4. Valuation
5. Agency
6. Negotiations
7. Location, location, location

Let's explore these differences.

1. Confidentiality: in a real estate listing you want to put a sign in the yard, post the property in multiple listings, on the Internet and elsewhere and put specific information in real estate publications given away at convenience stores and other locations. With the intent that you want *everyone* to know that a house or other real estate is for sale. In small business listings, there is a 180 degree difference. You do not want *anyone* to know that the business is for sale. Not the employees, not the customers, not the competition, nor the vendors, nor the landlords nor banks. It is none of their business that the business is for sale until it becomes their business with a pending sale of the business.

2. Financing: In the sale of a home there are hundreds of mortgage companies that will lend you at least 90 percent of the appraised value of the real estate, and if every house in a subdivision sells from a range of $160,000 to $195,000, I can pretty well tell you what a 3 bedroom, 2 ½ bath house, with a 1 car garage will sell for based on comparable sales in that area. That 90 percent financing helps to develop market value. The fact that so many lenders are willing to give homeowners a 90 percent loan to value (or more) underpins and upholds the value of the house.

Financing a business is again 180 degrees different. Banks do not make small business "acquisition" loans. They say they do, but they don't. Now, they'll lend you money once you own the business and have a proven track record of success - to buy equipment, to buy inventory - or they will make you a small loan to buy a delivery truck; however, they will not lend you several hundred thousand dollars to *buy* a business. This is for two reasons.

First, banks don't have any real security in a business loan. Unlike the home loan where if every house in the subdivision sells from $160,000 -$195,000 and if the bank lends you money and for whatever reason you take off, move to California, get hit by a truck, or for whatever reason, do not pay them, they could foreclose and resell the house for the loan balance and the mortgage security would pay the loan. A house does not require management the way an operating business does. It could sit empty for several months and would probably still sell for from $160,000 to 195,000.

Also, the bank's loss ratio experience in residential home loans in the U.S. is so low (under 6 percent) they can actually "bundle" home loan mortgages and sell them in what is called the "secondary market," such as Fannie Mae or Freddie Mack. That way they do not have their money tied up in the loan.

A business requires management; if the bank were to make you a business loan to buy a business and you take off or get hit by a truck, how would the bank get their money back? They cannot operate the business. If they foreclose on the business and close the doors on an operating business, the hard asset value of a business goes down to practically nothing. For instance, if you had a dry cleaner or a restaurant with $300,000 worth of equipment and you close the doors, the value of the equipment goes to maybe 10 cents on the dollar. You'll be lucky if you can give the equipment away. There is another problem. The rent is due, and landlords and other creditors may have dibs on the assets.

Every now and then, the banks look at the size of the small business market and say, "We have got to get into that market." However, small business lending has proven to be a very difficult arena for banks, even with SBA guarantees.

For five years running, the most aggressive small business lender in America was the Money Store based in Sacramento, California. In 1998, First Union Bank bought the Money Store; in 2000 they shut down the Money Store, laid off 3,000 employees overnight and wrote off $3 billion dollars in bad loans. They proved once again that when you have to foreclose on a small business loan it "ain't going to be pretty."

In November 2000, another very aggressive small business lender, Transamerica Small Business Capitol, shut down overnight and laid off all of their staff and got out of the business of small business lending. They were followed by Heller Financial in 2001.

When it comes to small business, banks do not really have any security. If the business model doesn't work; if the business does not produce earnings and a living for the owner, they know that the bank will not get paid. Good credit does not pay the loan payments; "cash flow" pays the loan payments.

Also, banks are risk-adverse. They do not want to take a risk that cannot be covered by security under the worst-case scenario. Their definition of security in a worst-case scenario is what assets the bank can seize, take to market within 30 days and sell and get their money back. Besides, banks usually define small business for their purposes as those doing from $3,000,000 to $20,000,000 in annual gross sales. So even though the banks take out full-page ads in the newspaper, and are on television saying that, "we are the small business lenders," they very seldom make small business *acquisition* loans. I would like to suggest that they take some of that advertising money and really make some small business loans!

Since the bank doesn't have any security in a business loan, they will not lend you the money. Unless of course you put up some outside security, such as your house, for instance. But your wife is probably too smart for that, and if she doesn't think it's a good idea to put up your house for security to buy a business, she'll probably stop you. And if she can't stop you, she'll call her daddy, and her daddy never really liked you very much anyway. So he says, "Put that boy on the phone right now, he is not putting my little girl and my grandchildren on the street for some crazy business deal! Tell that boy to get a job like I did!"

I don't blame your wife. I wouldn't put my house up for security to buy a business either; it's too much of a risk. A business ought to stand for its own security.

The second reason a bank will not finance a business is that they must have proven debt repayment ability. Your friendly banker will always say, "Bring in the last three years financials and tax returns on the business and we're ready to go."

However, if you bring in the tax returns, never stand in front of the banker. He'll probably "throw up" all over the floor because he's already told you he'd give you a loan and he can't figure out how in the world he's going to get paid back out of the financials. He's got to see enough money in the financials after taxes to repay the bank (which is the bank's main concern), and enough for you to make a living.

Seldom will the financials show that. They have been prepared for one main purpose: to pay no taxes, not to show how well the business is doing. So before it's over the bank will not lend you the money because they do not have security and they do not have proven debt repayment ability. Also, there is no reliable secondary funding sources for small business loans like Fannie Mae or Freddie Mac to "take out" the bank's investment.

Now if the bank or another lender can get an SBA guarantee, then there is the bank's security. The very fact that a lender will make the loan gives you a certain comfort level, in that they feel the business deal will work. The bank or lender has approved the financials and they feel that the business will continue to be successful. Now if they make you a loan and you get hit by a truck, get a divorce, take off for parts unknown or the business model doesn't work for whatever reason, the bank simply calls the security (SBA) for repayment.

Normally the SBA guarantee is at an interest rate of prime plus 2.25 to 2.75 percent. So it also costs more. However, with the SBA guarantee, the bank may lend the money. The SBA, however, always requires your house as additional security. They don't like risk either.

Now don't you have to have the same things in a home loan? In a home loan you have to have security and proven debt repayment. The security is in the property based on comparable market value, and debt repayment is your employment verification or proven income records.

For the same two reasons that a *bank* won't make the loan, the *seller* should make you the loan and the seller is in a far better position to finance the business.

First, security. If for some reason you didn't pay the seller, he could foreclose and take the business back over. Whereas the bank would simply close the doors and lose everything because they couldn't manage the business, the seller could step back in and take over the management of the business to protect his investment. He doesn't want to of course, but he could. The seller is in a far more secure position than the bank because he can run the business until he could sell it again.

And secondly; as far as the financials are concerned, who knows more about the actual "cash flow" or earnings of the business than the seller, for goodness sake? He or she has been running the business for years and providing for his or her family out of the business. Forget the financials and tax returns showing a loss, the seller knows better than anyone (and he is the only one who truly knows) whether the earnings of the business can allow for debt repayment to him or her and still leave enough money for the buyer and their family to live on.

So the very fact that the seller will lend you the money to buy the business (or that he *won't* lend you the money to buy the business) probably tells you more about the value of the business than anything else.

In fact, I personally believe very strongly in seller financing. I call it "the seller putting his money where his mouth is." He says, "I'm selling you a good business that I truly believe will continue to be successful and make you a living, Mr. Buyer, just like it has done for me. Therefore, I am willing to lend you part of the money to buy it."

Also, seller financing is important for this reason. Unlike an SBA loan that is prime plus 2.25 percent to 2.75 percent, seller financing is usually at prime rate or less, not more. The seller knows better than anyone how many dollars you can take out of the cash flow of the business each month to service the debt and still allow the buyer enough money to make a living.

Seller financing is so important to establish the real relationship of buyer to seller in the transaction that I tell my buyers, "If a seller won't finance part of the business sale, I don't believe I'd buy it." You know why I say that? I absolutely *believe* that! The best and only way to be assured that all of the information the seller is telling you about the business is true is for the seller to finance part of the purchase price. Owner financing levels the playing field between the buyer and the seller. It forms a solid bridge in the "leap of faith" between the buyer and seller necessary to put a deal together.

Now we occasionally have an "all cash" deal. Here is a way to give a buyer a way to get a comfort level even in an "all cash" purchase. Get the seller to agree to set aside 20 percent of the purchase price in the closing attorney's escrow account for 60 days after the closing to allow the buyer to properly transition the business and verify the seller's representations have been accurate.

3. Relationships: In the real estate business there is no relationship between the buyer and seller. The buyer gets a new mortgage, pays off the old mortgage and buys the house. Often, the buyer and seller do not even meet, or if they do meet it's for that one- hour "happy talk" meeting at the closing. The buyer and seller have no relationship.

Small business is 180 degrees different. *Relationships are every-*

thing! *Relationships are everything*! The relationship between the business broker and the seller, the relationship between the business broker and the buyer and the relationship between the buyer and seller.

If the seller is going to finance this sale for 5 years or 7 years or 10 years, there is going to be a 60, 84, 120 month relationship, respectively, between the buyer and seller. Both parties have a significant vested interest in the continued success of the business. Unlike real estate where the closing is the beginning and the end of the relationship. In business, the closing only *begins* the relationship.

4. Valuation: What is the value of something? Americans like a definition of value. We normally equate price with value. While shopping in a store, we pick out the items that we want, they run them through the scanner at the checkout and the total is the amount that we pay. In buying a car we look at the blue book value, in real estate we look at comparables. When it comes to valuing a business compared to valuing real estate the financing also plays a major part. As we discussed earlier, if every house in the subdivision sells from $160,000 to $195,000, I can tell you what a house would sell for by figuring that the banks will loan 90 percent plus of the sales price to a qualified buyer. That financing is a major underpinning of market value.

Think about this.

If there were no bank financing; what would a house sell for? Perhaps less, perhaps more. The actual answer is that it would sell for what a ready, willing and able buyer would and could pay and what a ready, willing and able seller would accept. In other words, it would be a true "market value" driven price.

In a business sale, because there is normally no bank financing to underpin the appraised value, a business will sell for what a buyer can and will pay and what a seller will take given a price and terms and conditions agreeable to everyone. That is the market that we are in – in business brokerage.

Now in this instance, small business value and large business value (publicly traded businesses) are similar. What is a business worth? What the market says it is today; right now, in fact if the stock exchange is open. You will see all kinds of legitimate approaches to the market value of a business. Multiple of earnings, multiples of EBIT (earnings before interest and taxes), and multiples of EBITDA (earnings before interest and taxes, depreciation and amortization). However, the real value is what the stock market says is it right now determined by what its shares of stock are selling for at the present time. And just as a lot of day traders and savvy investors found out, the price you paid several months ago might not be the same as the market value today. Check out Lucent Technology!

5. Rules of Agency: Business brokers almost always work for the seller. Our legal and fiduciary responsibilities are to the seller. However, we must honestly and fairly deal with the buyer, and we never work against the buyer. A business deal must work for a buyer or he/she won't buy and if the buyer doesn't buy, a seller can't sell. And the market sets the value.

A business deal needs to be a win-win situation for both the buyer and the seller or it won't work. We are normally not working with a foolish buyer or a foolish seller, nor do I want to be dealing with a foolish buyer or foolish seller. Also, there is very little co-brokering in business brokerage. This is primarily because of confidentiality issues. Normally the brokerage firm that lists a business also sells the business. So the rules of agency are somewhat different in explanation. However, we disclose our agency relationships to buyers and sellers, alike. Both must have confidence in the broker's fairness and honesty or they will probably not buy or sell. The business broker serves as a "finder" and a "facilitator." The broker does not warrant the correctness, completeness or accuracy of the information that the seller provides to the buyer about the business – it is up to the buyer to do their own due-diligence on the business and/or the seller. Likewise, the broker does not warrant the qualifications of the buyer: it is up to the seller to do their own due diligence on the buyer. The broker is like a preacher in a marriage ceremony – we perform the service of putting the two together; however, you cannot blame the preacher if the marriage doesn't work.

6. Negotiations: We as Americans are not comfortable negotiating. We think we are, but we are not. In almost all of our transactions, we equate price with value, and we either pay the price or we don't buy. It is perfectly normal and acceptable to just walk away; however, we have a cultural bias against negotiations.

If you were going through a checkout line at the grocery store or Wal-Mart or Kmart or Sears or Home Depot and the bill was $68.20, you wouldn't think of asking, "Would you take $40.00 cash for these items?" Nice people do not negotiate. If you do not believe that, try to negotiate at the next check-out line with your kids standing next to you. They will slowly move away from you without making eye contact, hoping that no one noticed and realized that you are their Daddy.

The only items that "nice people" can negotiate on comfortably are at flea markets, yard sales or when buying a car. However, every time they take a survey about what folks don't like about buying a car, guess what the number one answer is? The hassle of negotiating.

Now, in buying a business you have to negotiate. *Well,* you do not *have* to, but here is what I mean. Let's say that the seller is asking $200,000 with $100,000 down payment and you only have $40,000 in down payment ability. If you were going to buy the business, it would have to be no more than a $40,000 down payment and the seller would have to finance the balance or there will be no sale.

There is a major difference with a foreign buyer, however, because foreign buyers have a cultural bias *towards* negotiating. They come from a culture where everything is negotiable, and they are buying a lot of businesses because they negotiate and they make an offer. Approximately 20 percent of small business buyers are foreign buyers. Haven't you noticed how many convenience stores, liquor stores, coin ops, laundries and motels new Americans own? Indian buyers, Asian buyers, Middle Eastern buyers, South American buyers, Canadian, Mexican, and European buyers summarily dismiss the asking price and just make an offer. These new Americans have a strong motivation to buy a business because it is almost politically impossible to get a "work visa" to come to America. The government looks at that as taking jobs away from Americans. However, with an E-2 Visa or an L1 Visa, a "substantial investment visa," politically, the government views that as a way of investing in and adding to the economy and providing jobs and saving jobs and that is the ticket to America. But you can expect strong negotiations on price and terms.

7. Location, location, and location: In the real estate business (I have been in the real estate business in South Carolina since 1970), we always say the three most important things that influence value are location, location, and location. Well, in business, that is not necessarily true. The three most important things that influence value in a business are:

1) Location (depending on the type of business): A restaurant or convenience store or retail business's success may depend heavily on its location. A janitorial business or lawn care business could be located in a garage somewhere, and location may have little to do with its value.

2) Track Record: The very fact that the business has survived for three years or longer, has an established customer base, an existing cash flow, trained employees, a trend of sales and a product or service that has proven itself in the marketplace, is an important factor.

3) Management: Management is so important and so immediate in a business that you can have a good location and a good product or service, but if the management is not done correctly, the business will most probably not do well. Conversely, how many times have you seen a business, particularly a restaurant, go out of business, and six months later another food service business moves right in to that same location and "kicks the doors down" with business. Same location, same type of business – better management.

So using my sports analogy of big business (football rules), small business (baseball rules) and real estate (basketball rules) - they are all three ball games; however, the rules are very different, and we have to make sure that we are using the right rules for the right ballgame. Let's look at what rules are important to you.

Chapter 8
How Much Can I Make?

What does a buyer really want to know about a business? What does he really need out of the business? He or she needs an income! If I take this job…if I buy this business… if I buy this job… how much will I make? That is ultimately what a buyer wants to know.

The best answer to that is to determine how much the present owner is making less the new debt service paid to the seller or to the bank (if you were able to get a bank loan). The new debt service payment of the business has to come out of the existing cash flow.

So, how much does a business make? The best rule of thumb for that requires that we divide small business into two sections. Those that have annual gross sales of $1,000,000 per year **or less** and those that do $1,000,000 per year **or more**. From now on, let's forget big publicly traded business; we do not deal with them. Also, let's call a business doing $1,000,000 or less in annual gross sales a *small business* and those that do $1,000,000 or more a *big business* (both privately held).

Normally a business has sales growth of 3 to 15 percent a year. The earnings available to the managing owner of a small business is approximately 10 to 20 percent of the business's gross sales. For instance, if a business has $300,000 per year in gross sales, there is potentially $30,000 to $60,000 available to the owner. Gross sales of $400,000 per year would provide from $40,000 to $80,000 to the owner. I call that the true owner's net, the owner's discretionary cash flow or the recast earnings, or "normalized" earnings plus "perks." I believe the seller when he or she tells me he is making 10 to 20 percent of his gross sales, provided, of course, that he will finance part of the business purchase price based on his warranty and representation. If he would not finance part of the purchase price – I would not buy the business.

Once a business gets above $1,000,000 in gross sales, the earnings potential or the "true owner net" gets squeezed down to 10 percent of gross sales or less very quickly. Any business doing over $1,000,000 in gross sales whose owner is making anywhere near 10 percent of gross sales is doing well.

Whatever total lifestyle a business is providing to the owner and his or her family is what I call the "true owner net." True owner net is also what is available to a new owner for both new debt services and to live on.

Take a gift shop for instance, which has a "keystone mark-up," meaning you buy a wholesale product for $5.00 and sell it for $10.00. You double the cost.

Let's say the shop does $100,000 in gross sales.

$100,000 gross sales = 100% of sales

less - $50,000 cost of goods sold < - 50% cost >

= $50,000 gross profit

less - 30-40% (business expenses, non-discretionary expenses, such as, employee salary, rent, electric bill, phone bill, insurance, etc.)

= 10-20% left available to the owner as True Owner's Net (depending on how the owner manages the business)

Now factor in the effects and influence of tax management and expense out depreciation (there is no actual physical depreciation in a gift shop; it's a cash flow shelter); expense out your car, perhaps your spouse's car, auto insurance, health insurance, life insurance; expense out trips to the gift trade market in Atlanta, New York, London, San Francisco, etc, and perhaps even expense out a family member who gets a small salary or "allowance" for helping out at the store, and this business will probably show a loss for tax purposes. However, the "true owner's net," what's left to the owner after paying all non-discretionary expenses, the real owner benefit for owning the business, is between 10 and 20 percent of the business' gross sales.

Some businesses will outstrip the 20 percent rule for a while, then market forces usually correct it. For instance, the best cash flow business I've ever seen in twenty years of selling businesses was the video rental business when it first came out. It blew the top off the 20 percent rule.

The price of VCRs dropped from $1,200 to $200 over a short period of time, and everyone owned a VCR and rented movies like crazy. Remember the $49.95 lifetime membership cards? What a deal for the store owner. They put your name and address in a computer and gave you a membership card that cost 10 cents. Is that a great mark-up or what – $49.95 for a 10-cent card. Then they would sell you (rent you) a movie that you brought back and then was sold to the next member for the same rental factor with no additional cost of goods sold.

The video storeowners were taking money to the bank in wheel-barrows. Then the market began to get saturated with a video store on every corner, and Blockbuster Video came out and changed the dynamics of the entire industry. Blockbuster opened "mega stores"

(5,000 plus square feet, 10,000 titles) with neon signs in the window advertising "free" memberships with a video rental. They had used the favorite word in the English language - "free" - and with their ability to have large, beautiful, well-stocked and well-run stores open 24 hours a day, 7 days a week, coupled with national advertising, a strong brand name and stock market money, they quickly dominated the video rental market.

Remember when "they" said the movie theaters would soon go out of business? Well, now theaters are springing up like mushrooms after rain. Going out to the movies is an event; a "date night," and folks enjoy the change and getting out of the house.

However, between cable TV, satellite dish TV, home computers and people like my wife Elaine, who buys rather than rents movies after they come back down into the $9.95 range, movies don't get rented nearly as frequently as before. As smart as Mr. Sumner Redstone is, and I am sure he is a smart man, no one can stop a market trend change. Now Blockbuster is in trouble. Great locations, high rent, and compared to a few years ago, low sales. If it were not a publicly traded company with revenue of stock sales in addition to product or service sales, it would probably have gone out of business. And when you figure the true owner net on a video store you'll see it's back in the 10 to 20 percent range.

As for the movie theaters, what in the world were they thinking? The same guy who did the market study for the motel business must have done the market study for the theater business. "Let's build another 16-plex, 24-plex, 30-plex rocking chair theater in this suburb." These theaters are huge, they are very comfortable and they cost $1,000,000 per screen to build. When you go to the movies, there are 28 people in the theater. You can't make that up, even with a $15 bag of popcorn. Almost every major theater chain in America is in bankruptcy. Many are closing. The old rules still apply. You have to take in more in sales than it cost to operate your business or you will go out of business.

You also have to constantly adjust to the market changes and competition. Take the pizza business for instance. When Pizza Hut first started with "eat-in" pizza parlors, they *owned* the pizza business. Remember the unique roof designs and glass corners? Then Dominos came out and proved that the pizza business was a "delivery" business and Pizza Hut almost went broke trying to stick to their business model. Now Dominos *owned* the pizza business. Today, all of Pizza Hut's new stores are "take out and delivery."

Then the owner of Dominos made a bad business decision – he decided to become a sports mogul and he bought the Detroit Tigers and lost his focus on the pizza business. He almost went broke. Then he did a very smart thing. He sold the Detroit Tigers to the Little Caesars people. Now they have to run a sports team as well as the pizza business. The good news for Little Caesars is that they know more about the sports team industry – they also own the Detroit Red Wings.

These facts are exactly why I believe that a small business that has been in business three years or longer is a successful business. That it has made the necessary course corrections to survive and that the owner must be paying all of his business's bills and making enough in addition to be paying his house payment, car payment and feeding all his children three times a day. Where else is the money coming from? Out of the "true owners net" of the business, the real cash flow. Now, remember, you can go for years without a profit, but you cannot go a week without cash flow. (And it's probably better not to buy a sports team.)

Chapter 9
The CASH in Cash Flow

Now let's talk about the *cash* in cash flow! Many small businesses, under $1,000,000 in annual gross sales, operate on what I call "checkbook accounting." Revenues are deposited into the company's bank account or checkbook and expenses are paid out of the company's checkbook. There is one cash register, and the owner receives all income and pays all expenses. What accounting is done uses real "cash accounting" rather than the "accrual" method of accounting that larger businesses normally use. The owner's management style of "always being there" and the management's control of the money allow for the reasonable control of the business using one set of books based on the most important book, the checkbook.

On the 20th of every month a business has to file a sales tax return with the state tax commissioner, and almost every state has a sales tax (normally from 6 percent to 8.25 percent of gross sales). That percentage is the amount of taxes that is due and payable on the 20th of the month with the filing of the sales tax report. If Mom & Pop didn't have to file tax returns, they probably wouldn't do that much accounting.

This has never happened in Charleston, South Carolina; however,

I have heard of it happening in other parts of the country. Mom & Pop small business owners realize that if they don't report quite as much sales, they won't have to write quite as big a check to the state tax commissioner on the 20th of the month. For instance, if they report $100,000 in gross sales this past month, they have to include a check for $8,250 assuming the higher tax rate of 8.25 percent. Now if they only report $90,000 in gross sales, they don't have to write quite as large a check.

Having personally sold many businesses over the years, here is what I believe with all my heart. Whatever the business owner reported in gross sales and *paid sales tax on* - I believe he did *at least* that amount in sales and that is the number I can "hang my hat on" to arrive at the 10-20 percent "true owner's net" earning potential. If the owner represents to me and to the buyer that the cash flow or true owner's net is between 10-20 percent of his reported gross sales, I'll believe that. Provided, of course, that the seller will finance part of the purchase price based on the seller's warranty and representation. And if he wouldn't finance part of the purchase price, then I would not buy the business.

What, you say? How could they do that? How could they not keep complete and accurate books and perhaps not report all of their sales? Very well, thank you, is how - and they pay more than their fair share of taxes in other ways. Unlike big business that hires lobbyists to write the tax laws that allow them to expense out all kinds of lifestyle perks, Mom & Pop will have to survive in other ways. And if they are nothing else, small business owners are survivors. They have survived through start-up, they have survived the competition, they have survived theft from employees and customers, they have survived market changes and they have survived the tax man.

They do pay taxes; however, and lots of them. They pay taxes on their real estate property, on their autos, on the furniture, fixtures and equipment, on their inventory; they pay withholding taxes on their employees, unemployment taxes and they collect and pay sales tax on their reported sales, and they also pay sales taxes on everything they buy. They pay taxes on their salary. So you can see they pay more than their fair share of taxes.

But now, let's look at an example of cash management in a private business.

Say you and your wife own and manage a dry cleaning business. You open at 7:00 a.m. and you are in the store until 7:00 p.m. Today's receipts are $400 ($100 cash and $300 in checks and credit cards). Now actually, the real ratio is almost exactly reversed, $300 is in cash and $100 checks and credit cards, but for our example let's use the $100 cash when you close up. What a day!

Your wife says, "Let's pick up the kids and go out to eat. I'm too tired to cook," and you don't know how to cook. So you and the family head out to Applebee's or TGI Friday's, and supper costs $46.00. On the way home, you fill your car with gas or fill up your wife's car with gas and at home, one of the kids says he needs $20 for school tomorrow and another kid needs $15. Tomorrow, in the bank line, you have $308 in the bank bag so you figure you had better keep the $8 for lunch and you deposit $300 in checks and credit card receipts.

Now, fast-forward to the 20th of the month and you are filling out your sales tax report for this month. What do you think the "reported" sales for that day are going to be for tax purposes - $300 or $400? Remember, you have to send that check for 8.25 percent of the reported sales that day.

I'll bet that the reported sales will be $300 for that day. Now, go to Saturday of that week. The largest day of the week, with folks picking up their dry cleaning for the weekend. Let's say Saturday's sales reached $600 ($200 in cash and $400 in checks and credit cards). You put the $600 in the bank bag and head home. What a week!

You go grocery shopping over the weekend, take the kids to the park, and come Monday morning in the bank line, you have $400 in checks and credit cards for your deposit. Again, fast forward to the 20th of the month. What do you think the reported sales are going to be for Saturday? My guess is $400.

Now, I am not saying that it is right or wrong, but I am saying that it is often the way that the real world of small business works. Mom and Pop do not run that business to keep accurate books and pay taxes. They run that business to provide a living for themselves and their family.

This example allows for two days out of a six-day workweek. Multiply that by 52 weeks in a year and expand the example for every day of the week. That could amount to somewhere between $15,000 to $30,000 that never went into the business's bank account or check-book and therefore never went into the business's set of books.

In a bigger business, one with over $1,000,000 in annual gross sales, there is no cash that isn't being reported in the books. The big business has the same management style and accounting needs that General Motors does. You cannot keep up with the big business using checkbook accounting. You must operate with complete books, and you must close out everything on a regular basis. This is especially true with multiple locations in a business. Mom and Pop could not possibly keep up with a million dollar - plus business in their heads by just using checkbook accounting. They would lose control of the business and where they are, and if you lose control of where you are, your employees find out very quickly that you don't know where you are and then you *don't* know where you are. You may have some "partners" that you hadn't planned on, or didn't know you had.

Over a million in annual gross sales forces a business to have more complete books and therefore, you can recast the financials just like you do the Big Business (football) rules. It's all in there. Since the financials are still done to pay no taxes or to minimize taxes to allow for the owner's lifestyle, I still need to sit down with the owner and get him or her to show me where the "dogs are buried" in the financials. What money is discretionary cash flow? How much can be added back to the "real" bottom line and therefore, what is the true owner's net?

The books of a small business, under $1,000,000, are kind of like Prego spaghetti sauce. "If it ain't in there, it ain't in there."

You cannot recast the unreported cash if it never went into the bank and it never went into the books.

So, let's say that the owner of the dry cleaners is reporting $428,000 in gross sales (adding up the twelve months of reported gross sales), and he tells me that he is making $68,000 a year. I absolutely believe that. Based on my 10-20 percent rules you can make from $40,000 to $80,000 per year out of a business doing over $400,000 in gross sales. But if approximately $30,000 of the $68,000 was cash, I'll never be able to *prove* the total cash flow based on the business's books.

When he agrees to finance the purchase based on his warranty and representations, I'll believe him. If he refuses to finance part of the deal, I will not buy it.

As I stated earlier, small business pays more than its fair share in taxes and provides most of the jobs in America. Almost 100 years ago, Oliver Wendell Holmes wrote, "Taxes are what we pay for a civilized society." Yes, but today, all tax laws are written by special interest groups. Every year there are thousands of individuals and companies that have incomes exceeding $200,000 per year, and they legally pay no taxes.

In 1934, Judge Learned Hand wrote, "Anyone may so arrange his affairs that his taxes shall be as low as possible; he is not bound to choose the pattern which will best pay the Treasury. There is not a patriotic duty to increase one's taxes."

And I always liked Mr. Steve Forbes' presidential campaign proposal of a "flat tax." Congress will never pass a flat tax. Do you know why? Because there is a powerful and respected lobbyist group deathly against a flat tax. And they are not your ordinary tax evaders. They represent what are called "charitable deductions."

Churches, universities, colleges, hospitals, the Red Cross, Salvation Army and every other non-profit organization in the world. A large portion of their budget is based on charitable giving for which they can offer charitable tax deductions as incentive to donate money. And since they do not have to pay taxes, their "true owner's net" is always "before taxes." Now you and I always thought that rich folks who gave big money to the university and to charities were just nicer than we were. We never thought about the tax strategy.

And Steve Forbes has steadfastly refused to give out his personal tax returns. He said it would distort his message. I bet it would! I bet he doesn't pay any taxes or relatively few taxes, considering his worth. You see, rich folks have tax deductions and tax shelters that we have never heard of. That's why I don't get so upset when Mom and Pop small business owners do everything they can to "legally" lower their personal taxes. After all, they probably pay more taxes on profits than General Motors does.

When I first mention to new brokers in training or when educating a new buyer about the "real cash flow" of a business and how it may vary from what is shown on the business tax returns, they sometimes question the honesty of a small businessperson. Let's put this situation in the proper perspective, by using an analogy.

If I had a family farm and on that farm I raised some corn, wheat, peaches, cows, hogs and chickens, you wouldn't even question the fact that the eggs my family and I had for breakfast this morning came right out from under the chickens. I did not pay retail for the eggs and they never showed up in my family's farm books. Neither did the corn, wheat and peaches my family ate. I run this farm to provide for my family, not to keep books or pay more taxes than necessary. If I started off this year with 10 cows and they had 4 calves and I ended up with 10 cows because my family and I ate 4 of them you wouldn't think anything was wrong with that, would you? They were my cows!

And if one of my daughters sold some peaches from a small roadside stand and made $350 over the summer for a school trip to Washington that didn't get into the family's farm books; what would be wrong with that? If we decided to trade some produce for products or services, what would be wrong with that? And we also raised our own vegetables and feed for our livestock.

Now when we harvested the corn crop, and sold it to ADM or the Co-op and got a check for $37,825 and a check for the wheat crop for $49,715 and the peaches brought in a check of $18,023, all of that we deposited in the bank. The farm's books were based on that deposited revenue minus any and all expenses, and depreciation and any and all legal deductions that constitute my family farm's financials. And sure enough, we lost money again, for the eleventh straight year. The personal consumption never went into the books; however, it certainly helped to provide a lifestyle for my family and me. Which is exactly what a family farm is supposed to do.

Since most folks do not have a family farm, the family business *is* the family farm. And they run their business to provide for themselves and their family, just like our grandfathers and grandmothers did when they raised, fed and educated a family of five out of the corner grocery store that they lived over. You better believe that store never showed a profit for tax purposes; however, it did exactly what a family business is supposed to do, it provided for the owner and his or her family.

Today's family farm is a dry cleaners or a grocery store, a retail business, a restaurant, lounge, convenience store or auto repair business, and it's run just like the family farm. If junior comes home from school and needs a new pair of Nike shoes for basketball practice, Dad takes the money right out of the cash register. Sis's piano lessons are paid for in cash or traded out of the business, and the owner's car, wife's car, gas, auto insurance, health insurance, life insurance, is all paid for through the business with *before* tax dollars, not *after* tax dollars.

The business convention often doubles as a family vacation trip, and the family business provides the total family lifestyle for the family, just like a family farm used to.

The 10-20 percent true owner net formula of cash flow allows for the "cash" in cash flow. It doesn't matter to me if an owner takes out his money in a paycheck, cash, or family perks, the total amount available to the owner of a business for cash flow could be between 10-20 percent of gross sales. I wouldn't believe anybody who tells you he is making more than 20 percent on his gross sales, unless he is selling cocaine or something on the side.

For instance in the food service industry, there is a ratio of 28-32 percent on food costs, 28-32 percent labor costs, and 5-10 percent rent, another 10 percent for some additional costs such as advertising, electric bill, telephone bill, insurance, leaving available to an owner a true owner net of from 10-20 percent of gross sales depending on management.

So to restate an important point, if an owner (seller) of a small business represents to me or to you that he or she is making between 10-20 percent of gross sales (and a larger business, 10 percent of gross sales), I'll believe that, provided that they will finance the purchase of the business based on the warranty and representation. And if he or she won't finance part of the purchase price, I would not buy the business!

Chapter 10

Buyers

Most buyers of businesses in America today are not entrepreneurs in the true sense of the word. Entrepreneurs are "risk takers." *Risk?* I don't want to take any risks! This is my life savings for goodness sake. This investment *has* to work! I've found that most buyers are what I call "forced entrepreneurs." They probably have a better chance of making a good living for themselves and their families going into business for themselves than they do just getting another job, especially if they are over forty years old. As we mentioned earlier, there are not a lot of $70,000 to $80,000 per year jobs out there in today's economy. To make that kind of money, you probably need to own your own business.

A motivated buyer is probably not one who has a job, but says, "I always wanted to own my own business." A truly motivated buyer is probably one who doesn't have a job and is burning through his $60,000 in life savings. Every month he delays finding another job or starting or buying a business, he has about $4,000 less in savings. The next month he has $56,000, the next month he has $52,000, then $48,000 – that's a motivated buyer and he probably fits the profile.

Here is a list of what I like to call 90% Rules of Buyers; some of which were written by Tom West and some that I have added over the years. I try to do all of my training and educating on what I call 90% rules – most of the time they will bode you well.

Just like if you are a golfer, 90% of the time you do better when you stay within the fairways, don't you? Here are my *90% Rules of Buyers*:

1. 90% of buyers are first time buyers. In other words, they have not been in business for *themselves* before. They are not risk takers and they are not just investors.

2. 90% of buyers will have to *finance* the purchase price of a business, just like we had to finance the purchase of a house, a car, a boat or most other big-ticket items.

3. 90% of buyers are *not sure* what type of business to buy or what best serves their needs.

4. 90% of buyers are *scared to death* because owning their own business is new to them. For the first time in their adult lives, they don't have a job and if the husband is afraid, the wife is petrified. ("How are we going to make the house payment, the car payments, feed and educate the children, etc?")

5. 90% of buyers will have to get the *sellers to finance* part of the purchase price. So if you look at #2 – 90% of buyers will finance the business – where's the financing coming from? The seller, whether they want to be the source of financing or not.

6. 90% of buyers will *not buy* the business that they called about – they are just starting the process of elimination. And most decisions, big and small, are a constant process of elimination.

7. 90% of buyers have from $15,000 - $60,000 in the "Hip National Bank" that they are *willing to risk* or spend investing in a business. They may have a net worth of considerably more, such as owning a house valued at $300,000 with only a $100,000 mortgage; owning stocks or bonds that they do not want to sell at the present market or having $100,000 plus in a 401K retirement account. All of which add to their net worth, but none of which a buyer will normally wish to risk to buy a business.

8. 90% of buyers are used to and are very comfortable making what I call a *10% decision*. They'll pay 10% down on a house or car and as long as they can make the payments affordable, they don't care what the price is. However, buying a business is going to take most of their life savings and most of their time and attention. Therefore, it is not a 10% decision; it is much closer to a 100% decision. It's kind of like getting married. It's a 100% decision and that is one reason why it is so scary.

9. 90% of buyers are from *35 to 55 years old* and have come out of middle management with a company and are used to making from $45,000 to $95,000 per year.

The good news is that I believe that you can sustain a lifestyle comparable to an income from a job of $45,000 to $95,000, less tax, out of most of the existing businesses and franchises in America today. Provided that they have been in existence three years or longer and have a successful track record with annual sales growth from 3 to 15 percent or more.

You know why I am comfortable saying that? The present owner has a house payment, car payments, children to feed and educate just like you do, and he or she has been paying bills successfully right out of the existing business. How do you think they have been sustaining their lifestyle? In the real world, I believe that you can make a living for yourself and your family out of owning this business for the very reason that the present owner has been making a living for himself and his family out of the business for several years.

All things considered, if you buy this existing business, and you continue to run it as the present owner has been running it, you should be able to make the same living (income) less the new debt service, of course. The new debt service, whether it is paid off to the seller or to the bank, or to the SBA, has to come out of the business's earnings or cash flow. Where else can it come from?

So, when you are negotiating to buy a business, both the buyer and seller must be aware that the new debt service has to come out of the "real" cash flow or true owner's net and still leave the buyer enough money to live on, or the deal will not work; it will "crash and burn." And neither the buyer nor the seller wants that to happen.

In negotiating a business deal there are many things that are important, but none more so than the price and terms. Part of the price and terms is the all-important *down payment*. This is a "down payment driven business," and by and large the down payment is influenced much more by how much money the buyer has and will risk than it is by how much the seller wants or how valuable the business is.

In the real world a buyer cannot pay more money down than he/she has or can raise, no matter how much the seller wants. Unless there is bank financing, and most of the time there isn't, the amount of the down payment is driven by the buyer.

And there is nothing magic about the terms and conditions of the balance. The monthly payments have to come out of the cash flow of the business.

So if a seller represents to you that he is making $50,000 per year out of the business and that number fits into my 10-20 percent rule (in other words the business is doing at least $250,000 to $500,000 in reported gross sales) then you can believe him, provided he would finance the purchase. However, you cannot agree to pay the seller $3,000 per month payments just because that's what he wants.

You cannot take $3,000 per month debt service payments out of a business that makes $50,000 per year, unless of course you can live off $14,000 per year (which you can't). You are setting up a deal that will not work for either party, buyer or seller. The monthly payments have to be payable out of the cash flow leaving the buyer enough money to live on, or it won't work. Unless of course the buyer can increase the business or better manage the business to get additional true owner's net.

Also, the down payment should never take a buyer out of cash. He must have some working capital to carry the business for a while, even though an existing business should have an immediate cash flow. You also have to make a house payment, car payment, educate and feed your children. Although the seller always wants more down payment and the buyer always would like a smaller down payment, somewhere in between the two there is a fair deal, a level playing field, that will work for both parties, or we won't have a sale.

Since you cannot put out a sign on the business that says, "For Sale," as you do with real estate, and since there is no multiple listing service for business sales because of confidentiality – how do you find a good business for sale? Often when you look in the "Business Opportunities" section of the newspaper or under the "For Sale By Owner" you will be kind of "bottom fishing." Most good businesses are not listed under "For Sale By Owner."

My suggestion is to contact a business broker - just as you would normally get a good real estate broker to help you find the right house and a good stock broker to help you buy the right stocks. The business broker has hundreds of businesses for sale in all types of industries; retail, service, manufacturing, distribution, food service, dry cleaners, coin laundries, liquor stores and franchises. And since buyers normally pay no fees, the services of a business broker are free to a buyer.

Obviously, I recommend calling a Sunbelt Broker in your town because I trained them; plus, they have continued professional education as members of our industry trade association, the International Business Brokers Association (IBBA), and many of them have obtained the industry certification of Certified Business Intermediary (CBI).

If you cannot locate a local Sunbelt Business Broker, I recommend calling another member of the IBBA, since all members subscribe to the organization's Code of Ethics. I am confident that, while business brokers almost always work for the seller, they will treat all parties fairly and honestly and assist buyers in finding the right business. Because if a buyer doesn't buy a business, the seller can't sell a business, and remember that a deal *must work* for both the buyer and seller or it won't work.

Normally, you will find business brokers listed in the yellow pages of your phone book under "Business Broker," and you will find specific businesses for sale in your Sunday paper under "Business Opportunities" or "Businesses for Sale." If a broker runs the ad on the business, the ad must state that and identify the broker or the brokerage firm handling the sale.

Another way of finding a business for sale is on the Internet. This is the closest thing business brokers have to a multiple listing service to market the businesses they have for sale. However, because of confidentiality, you probably will never be able to look at an ad in the newspaper or on the Web that completely and specifically identifies the business.

Add to that these 90 percent rules that buyers do not know what kind of business they want or will best serve their needs and 90 percent of the time they are not going to buy the business they first call to inquire about and 90 percent of the time they do not know anything about baseball (small business) rules - and you come back to the same advice. Call a business broker and find one with whom you feel comfortable and who takes the time to meet with you, gets to know you and encourages you to get to know him or her and educates you about the real world of small business.

Again, in that recommendation I'm suggesting the same thing that I would if I were recommending you buy a house or buy stocks. Find a broker that you are comfortable with and ask their assistance in finding the right house or investment. Even though the real estate brokers normally work for the seller, they know the market, they know about financing and they can help you walk through the maze much better than you could wandering through it on your own.

Also, don't be a "day trader." Work with a broker – certainly express your preferences and help direct the broker to your wishes, but you will normally be far better off taking advantage of the professional broker's experience and knowledge. And he has hundreds of businesses to choose from.

The meeting with the broker and the meetings later with the seller must be *face to face*. Buying a business is too important and personal to be done over a fax machine or by phone or e-mail. All of the technologies may have some application and may save some time and facilitate the sales process. However, relationships take time to build and must be personal.

Occasionally, when I am talking with a buyer he'll say, "Just fax me the information on the business, or just fax me a Confidentiality Agreement and I'll fax it back." I won't do it; it just won't work that way.

I cannot help you find the best business for you without meeting you in person and trying to accomplish four very important things.

1. *I need to get to know you*, your background, your preferences, your lifestyle, your financial needs and your comfort level of financial risk.

2. *You need to get to know me*, my experiences, my background, my understanding of the industry, the marketplace, businesses for sale, and the available financing resources and the latest trends in business.

3. I need to *take the time to educate you* about the real world of small business. Almost nothing in your background can prepare you for small business (baseball rules). There are no absolute rules of value, there is no bank financing, the financials never look good, you've got to make an offer to get started and negotiate, etc., etc.

4. I need to get you to *sign a Confidentiality Agreement* requesting you to keep all of the information that I give to you about a specific business confidential and to keep confidential the fact that the business is even up for sale.

Now, all four of these things are very important; however, if you had to pick the least important, which one would that be? You may have guessed it, but if not, the answer is number four, the Confidentiality Agreement.

The other three things, all of which I consider to be most important, can be accomplished only with a face-to-face meeting. It is just like looking at a business, you have *got* to go see it and if you have any interest at all, you have to meet with the seller face-to-face to let him or her tell you about the business; how they got started in the business, what's presently going on, about the future of the business and why they are selling.

So much of this decision is going to be based on your "gut feelings" about the broker, the business and the seller, and the only way to have enough information is through personal meetings and exchanging a lot of information and asking a lot of questions.

I would not deal with a broker or a seller who would not meet with me and take the time to help me in all aspects of this major decision. If you cannot arrive at a comfort level with the broker, the business and the seller, then I would not recommend buying the business.

Remember that you are the buyer, you are the customer, and ultimately the buyer drives the deal. If the deal doesn't work for you and you don't buy it, then the seller has not sold it. So the first thing to accomplish is to find a broker you are comfortable with, then find a business you are comfortable with - one that you feel you can manage with the proper training and transition from the seller or the franchisor. Then get an accountant and a lawyer that you feel also comfortable with and follow the next steps covered in the chapters that follow.

If you do not go through a broker, you still have to have a comfort level with the seller and, of course, the business, and I'll show you how to protect yourself throughout the process. However, I always recommend a business broker because he/she understands the process, has a good knowledge of the local market and can help you navigate the many obstacles and work out a deal structure that works for you and for the seller.

Chapter 11
FOCUS Is Very Important

Throughout the business buying process, I ask my buyers to keep their *focus on the business, not on the financials*. The financials have been done with one purpose in mind, to pay no taxes or to minimize taxes. They have not been prepared to show how well the business is doing or to even be a fair portrayal of the value of the business. In fact, they have been done for just the opposite, to show that the business is not doing well for IRS purposes. I cannot change that fact, and I cannot change the financials. They are set in concrete. What I can change, hopefully, is the buyers understanding of what he or she is looking at when studying the financials.

"Well, can't you recast the financials like they do in Big Business," you say, "and rebuild the Seller's Discretionary Cash Flow, the EBIT or EBITDA?" Yes, but you cannot recast the "cash" or the "owner's perks" that never went into the financials in the first place. You cannot add back what is not in the financials. Remember the Prego spaghetti sauce reference, "If it ain't in there, it ain't in there."

The second area of focus is when we finally do see the financials; focus on the *top line; not the bottom line*. The only thing the bottom line on business financials reveals is that the seller has a good accountant or he doesn't. The top line tells me a great deal about the business. The top line (gross sales) tells me the market's response to the business's product and/or service. It tells me the trends of sales and it tells me if there is a large enough top line, based on my 10-20 percent rule, to give me enough of a bottom line to live on and to pay back my debt service.

Another example about the usefulness of the top line is this: at Sunbelt, I've done many appraisals for the courts. I have been certified as an expert witness on business valuation in dozens of court cases. Often times when there is a divorce situation or something and the husband and wife are fighting over the value of a business, the judge or the attorneys need an expert opinion on the value of the business.

Usually the husband goes into court with the financials and the tax returns and holds up the tax returns and says, "Your Honor, this business is not worth anything; here are my tax returns for last year, we lost $16,000." The judge is a lawyer, of course, and lawyers don't know anything about the value of a business, so he thinks, "Wow, they lost $16,000. I don't see how this poor devil is still in business."

Then, of course, the wife gets a chance to speak and she says, "Your Honor, I do not know anything about the financials, but I'll tell you this - Judge, this is a very valuable business. It has been the only source of income for our family for the last 15 years and we've always lived in a nice house, driven nice cars, taken a vacation every year, and sent our children to college and even gave this bum extra money to run around with his _____!" *"Order, order in the court!"* yells the Judge.

You know what? They are both telling the truth. The business is a very valuable business; it has provided a good living for the family for years, and it lost $16,000 for tax purposes this past year. When you are looking for value, look at the top line, not the bottom line.

The 10-20 percent rule is also a very real constraint. You can make $50,000 out of a business that is doing $250,000 - $500,000 per year in gross sales; you cannot make $50,000 out of a business that is doing $100,000 in gross sales.

The third area of focus is what I call the *70%-30% ratio*. Most of the weight of the buyer's decision (70 percent) should be based on what the buyer feels he or she could make based on how they would run or manage the business *after* they buy it. The smaller weight of the decision (30 percent) should be based on how the seller *has run* the business over the past few years.

For instance, if you are looking at an existing dry cleaning business: what can you do about how the seller has run the business for the last several years? Not one thing. Look at what you can change to make the business better. How would you run the business if you owned it? That is what you need to focus on.

Here is an example about a dry cleaner. Let's say that you are having a buyer/seller meeting and you ask the seller, "Mr. Seller, I noticed that you don't have a drive-through drop off at your dry cleaners. Do you think it would be a good idea to put in a drive-through?" The seller will probably reply to the effect of "I've thought about a drive-through, however the building configuration doesn't lend itself well to a drive-through and besides, my customers know that I don't have a drive-through so I don't believe it would make any difference."

Oh yeah? There are a lot of people, women in particular, traveling with small children or animals in the car who are just not going to stop at a dry cleaners that doesn't have a drive-through, especially in bad weather.

Another question might be: "Mr. Seller, I notice that you close at 6:00 p.m. Do you think it would be a good idea to stay open a little later?" The seller says, "I get here by 6:30 a.m. and by 6:00 p.m. I am tired and I want to go home and besides my customers know that I have always closed at 6:00, so I don't think that it makes any difference."

Oh yeah? In a lot of families, both the husband and the wife are working outside the home and with the rush hour traffic in the city, they don't even get home until after 6:00 p.m. and therefore they don't stop at your dry cleaners because they could only pick up their clothes on Saturday.

Mr. Sam Walton figured that out years ago. He said, "You know what? It seems a lot of families have both the husband and wife working all day so they don't have time to do the shopping between 9 and 5. We need to keep all of the Wal-Mart stores open late enough to let folks get home from work, feed the children and then go out shopping. We need to keep all of our stores open until 9 p.m., then 10 p.m., then 12 a.m. and some stores are open 24 hours."

Mr. Sam did something pretty radical. He decided to run his business based on *what his customers wanted*, not what he wanted. Because of that fact, he sucked up all of the business. The Mom and Pop stores that said, "We have always closed at 5-6 p.m.; our customers know that, it plainly says that on the door" – they are now permanently closed. More on Mr. Sam later.

One other question for the seller might be, "Mr. Seller, have you ever sent out any coupons in your market area?" He'll probably say, "No" or "Yes, we did that once in 1998, it seemed to work, but it's a little bit of a pain to keep up with." He might say, "You probably ought to do that. If I were just starting out, I would probably do it. Another question for the seller is, "Do you attend the industry trade shows?" Probably not.

Guess what? The buyer buys the business after some serious negotiations, with owner financing. He takes over new management, and he is full of enthusiasm.

He puts in a drive-through by laying those little drive over "ding-a-ling" bumpers that allows him to come out to a customer's car if they want and to pickup orders, give receipts, deliver orders and pick up payments at curb side. He stays open one more hour until 7:00 p.m. to allow folks to pick up clothes or drop off clothes on their way home. And he sends out coupons to every household within a five-mile radius of his store by zip codes. He adds wedding dress preservation to his service, and alterations, and valet service to surrounding hotels/motels. He learned how to do all of this efficiently at the industry trade shows.

The coupons announce that XYZ Dry Cleaners now has a "drive-thru" and that they are open until 7:00 every night for your convenience, Monday "thru" Saturday and that they have a special on shirts for the next 60 days.

Guess what, again? What do you think is going to happen to the sales of the business? Yep. They are going up with a very small increase in costs. The new buyer is paying the same amount of rent, same employee costs (he and/or his family are the only employees staying there to work the extra hour), the same FF&E (furniture, fixtures and equipment), but he is growing his top line, which gives him more of a bottom line.

So most of the weight of the decision to buy the business (70 percent) should be focused on what the buyer is going to do with the business *after* the sale. The new buyer often brings fresh enthusiasm to add to the old owner's experience and there is nothing better than enthusiasm. Even the word enthusiasm is good – it's derived from the Greek word meaning "with God."

You pay the seller for what he is doing with the business now, not based on the potential. However, you buy the business because of the potential.

Here is a very simple, one-page "Business Plan" for a small business that focuses on the business, the top line and what you would do to improve the business. I suggest you use it on any business you are looking at, and certainly you can expand it as needed. I like one-page plans, one-page agreements, one-page contracts and one-page letters.

SUNBELT®
BUSINESS
BROKERS

BUSINESS PLAN FOR

(Name of Business)

I. List five things about the business that you would continue to do:

1.
2.
3.
4.
5.

II. List five things about the business that you would change or
eliminate to improve the business:

1.
2.
3.
4.
5.

III. Variable True Owner's Net (dependent on your management):

Gross Sales X 20% = _____ (High range)
Gross Sales X 10% = + _____ (Low range)

Total _____ *Divided by 2 (Average)* = _____

Plus any employee salaries you and/or your family
would be picking up.   + _____

Less any note payments back to seller for financing. - _____

Your True Owner Net   _____

IV. Why would this be a good business for me?

Think about that one-page analysis. As I keep pointing out, the single most important decision that you make in life is whom you are going to marry. You don't sign a 58-page contract drawn up by the smartest lawyer for the most important contract in your life. Where are you going to live? Will you have children? How many children? What are you going to do? What is your spouse going to do? Who knows! You simply "show up," walk down the aisle in front of a broker (preacher or justice of the peace) and say, "I do."

It takes a 58-page agreement to "get out" of a marriage; however, my point is that the simplest agreements are often the best because the people have to make the contract work after the deal. No matter what is in the agreement, it's what is in your heart and head, not just the words on the paper. You have to work hard to make the deal work!

In every partnership contract I write I add the phrase that "all parties to this contract will use their best efforts and talents, both learned and God-given to make this a successful venture for all parties involved." While it is not legally binding, it goes to the spirit of the agreement, which is most important. As we go forward in this relationship just as in marriage, we cannot possibly "spell out" all the possible circumstances that may occur. Let's just agree to do our very best to work together to make things work for everyone.

Let's look at some small business that worked *Big Time*.

Chapter 12
War Stories

So many big businesses started out as small businesses and, through a series of management "course corrections," one business would do very well and another business in the same industry would not do as well. Let's look at some of those business stories, which I call "War Stories."

Every business has a story, just as every person has a story. And there is a lot more to a business story than just the financials. The financials are only one small chapter.

For instance, an important chapter in the story of a business might be the location. Another chapter might be the FF&E (furniture, fixtures and equipment) that produced the product or service; another chapter might be the inventory that the business sells. Another important chapter would be the one about employees. How many times have you heard the expression "the main assets of the business walk out the door everyday at 5 p.m.?" That's the employees. Still another chapter would be the industry itself and the future of the business in the industry. The trend of sales would be a chapter, as would a discussion of the competition. A major chapter would be on price and terms of a business's sale and, oh yes, one very important chapter would address the financials of the business, but that would be only one chapter, as I have already pointed out. I used to call the financials chapter, "Chapter 7," but that is a bankruptcy chapter so let's call the financials chapter "Chapter 6." That sounds a whole lot better.

One of the problems in seeking the advice and counsel of an accountant or in attempting to get a bank loan is that oftentimes, the accountant and the banker are only looking at Chapter 6 – only one chapter in the business story book to make decisions – they miss the "rest of the story" as Paul Harvey says.

Here are a few business success stories that have a lot more to do with the management /owners than they do with just the financials.

Story #1: Sam Walton; Wal-Mart

I had the pleasure of visiting Mr. Sam's original store, Walton's 5&10 in downtown Bentonville, Arkansas, about 3:30 a.m. one morning when I was nearby doing the opening training for the Sunbelt office in Fayetteville. (My friends Carl and Kathy Grimes own the Sunbelt office in Fayetteville, and they are a perfect example of why there is so much success through good people and good relationships, business and personal, in Northwest Arkansas.) I called my wife Elaine when I got in (as I always do) and told her I had just seen Sam Walton's original store and that I had finally arrived in Fayetteville. It was 4:30 a.m. in Charleston, and she didn't seem nearly as excited about my seeing Mr. Sam's store and the Wal-Mart home office as I was. She politely suggested that I call her later and tell her all about it. She also gave me a copy of Mr. Sam's book, *Made in America*, and some of what follows is paraphrased from Mr. Sam and some was garnered from watching Wal-Mart grow.

Mr. Sam said that he had never had an original thought and that he constantly sought ideas from other retailers and "stole or borrowed" the best ideas he found. He was a constant observer of business when it came to making "course corrections." Sam did not invent retailing; he did not invent discounting. When he first started, Sears or Kmart could have squashed him like a bug.

Mr. Sam started out as a licensee or franchisee of Ben Franklin Stores, and when he couldn't get a store where he wanted to live (Northwest Arkansas), he decided to go into business for himself. He liked Bentonville because of the local folks, and the other small towns that he could expand to. He also liked the fact that there are three states that meet together in that area (Arkansas, Oklahoma and Missouri) that (with a staggered bird hunting season) allowed a good living, a good place to raise a family - and a good place to hunt.

One of the main problems he and other retailers and particularly "discount" retailers had was "stealage," "shrinkage" or whatever else you want to call employee and/or customer theft. They did not have electronic monitors like they have today at every exit door.

When you did catch someone stealing, instead of just solving a problem, you began a new problem. You made an entire family of customers mad. When you catch a customer stealing, his or her dad comes down to the store, furious, ranting and raving, "My son wouldn't steal anything from your stupid store," and of course you have to say, "I know he wouldn't, but he had a lot of stuff accidentally stuffed under his jacket when he was leaving." Fortunately and unfortunately you caught a shoplifter, but you lost him, his parents, aunts, uncles and cousins as customers.

Out of the several stores that Mr. Sam operated, he had one store in particular that had considerably less shrinkage. Mr. Sam flew down in his plane to pay that store's manager a visit and see what this manager was doing right or differently from what the other managers were doing. You want to know what the secret weapon was? A greeter. He had a "greeter" at the door of his store.

Now shrinkage is probably not why the store manager had hired the friendly retiree to greet shoppers at the door. A lot of times in business, as in life, you make a minor change that results in a major course correction. The original greeter was a retired veteran, and he probably talked the manager into giving him a minimum wage position to help around the store with whatever odd jobs needed to be done to allow him to get out of the house. Everyone at Wal-Mart was paid minimum wage at that time.

However, being friendly by nature and probably knowing most of the folks in the town who shopped, when his chores were all finished, the vet headed to the front door and greeted customers as they walked in. "Good morning." "Good afternoon." "How are you all doing today?" "Thanks for shopping with us."

Mr. Sam considered the greeter to be the single best business idea he ever got. When you look someone in the eye and pleasantly welcome them into the store and thank them for shopping, two things magically happen. First, they think "the person who greeted me saw me come in here and could recognize me. I'd better not steal anything from this store." Secondly, the customers realize that these people are nice and that if they are going to steal something, maybe they'll go down the street and steal from the other store that doesn't take the time to say hello and be nice to its customers.

Either way, it worked! Mr. Sam put a greeter in every store immediately, either a retired man or lady, and shrinkage went down as front door customer relations went up. Less shrinkage went directly to Wal-Mart's bottom line and gave them a real advantage over the competition.

Then followed another small, but ultimately powerful, human

relations course correction at Wal-Mart. Mr. Sam noticed that the minimum wage employees were not outgoing or very effervescent; they were somewhat introverted and reserved. Even so, they were careful to follow company policies. So Wal-Mart set up this company policy: if a customer comes within 10 feet of an employee, the employee should greet them, ask them if they need any assistance or thank them for shopping Wal-Mart.

Wow! Look at the difference between a Wal-Mart and a Kmart in that one seemingly small, but important area. If you ask someone in Kmart where something is, you usually are interrupting, because they are busy doing something else. You have to hunt an employee down and say, "Excuse me, excuse me, but can you tell me where X is?" Probably they can't, but if they do happen to know where the item is, they'll say, "I think it's on aisle 14," and then they zoom back to whatever important mission they were working on before you came along.

When you ask someone in Wal-Mart where something is, you know what they'll do? They will take you to the item personally and then thank you for shopping.

One of the above-mentioned companies has constantly been on the brink of bankruptcy and recently did file for bankruptcy protection, under Chapter 11. The other is the largest retailer in the world. They are both discounters, they are both known-name "mega-stores," they both sell Igloo coolers and Coca Cola and Pepsi, they both have state of the art point of check-out inventory systems, distribution systems and great buying power. The difference is in the management.

Another major difference between Wal-Mart and Kmart is that Mr. Sam stocks his stores in the daytime, while customers are in the store. This means more employees to interact with customers, and "activity begets activity." Kmart stocks their stores at night, after hours. When you go in to shop in the morning at Kmart the store is neatly well stocked, but there are no people around to say "good morning."

One other difference among giant retailers that I find fascinating has to do with Sears. Before Wal-Mart really started growing, the largest retailer in the U.S. was Sears, and Sears has steadfastly refused to have one small item present in their stores: *shopping carts*. Think about it. When you shop at Sears, once you have an item in one hand and another item in the other hand and you can't carry anything else, you are done shopping. You are heading to the checkout and out to the car. If you are shopping with a small child or several small children, once you have your only free hand filled, you are done shopping. At Wal-Mart, Kmart, Home Depot, the local grocery store, etc., they all have shopping carts so that you can shop freely and don't have to be limited in your purchases by what you can carry. You can even put a toddler in the shopping cart, which makes for a more pleasant shopping experience.

Now why all the MBA geniuses in the Sears Tower in Chicago can't figure that one out, I'll never know, except that they still do not allow shopping carts. I guess they are counting on people with multiple sets of arms, bigger shopping bags and stronger biceps. Maybe they need to put a housewife on their board of directors.

And one other major difference in the success of Wal-Mart over its competition goes to the very heart of this book. Wal-Mart is a family business. Wal-Mart has an "owner family" that we can relate to. We shop at Mr. Sam's store and we feel like we know his family. His wife and children, his brother "Bud" and the rest of his family are all a major part of the Wal-Mart success story.

Who owns Kmart anyway? Who owns Sears? Faceless stock-holders. We don't know who the ever-changing management team is either. They aren't business owners, they are hired management folks. We feel that we know the people who own Dell Computer, Microsoft, Charles Schwab, AOL, CNN, McDonald's, Kentucky Fried Chicken,

Wendy's, Ben & Jerry's, and we know their stories. We can relate to them as regular folks just like us, who owned a family business and made it big. Good for them, and good for us! Americans love winners and success stories. We in turn support them with our business and our loyalty.

Story #2: Colonel Harland Sanders, Kentucky Fried Chicken

While I was driving up Interstate 75 to do the opening training for Brian and Stephanie Mazar, who are the Sunbelt office owners in Louisville and Lexington, Kentucky, I noticed a sign reading "Corbin, Kentucky, 2 miles." Recognizing Corbin as the birthplace of Kentucky Fried Chicken, I decided to visit the Colonel's original store.

Do you know why Col. Sanders started Kentucky Fried Chicken? The Highway Department built an Interstate Highway, I-75, and it missed his motel and restaurant on U.S. Highway 25 in Corbin, by about two miles. It put him out of business. Did he stop? No, he made a course correction. He auctioned off his motel and restaurant and barely got enough money to pay off his debts and mortgages. Then he and his wife took his first Social Security check proceeds and went "on the road" selling recipes for a special way of cooking chicken that everyone in the world would like. The rest, as they say, is history.

One life and business touches a lot of others, doesn't it? Col. Sanders was no exception to that rule, although he certainly was an exception. One of the folks he touched is another great businessman and a wonderful person (or at least seems to be, as I didn't get the pleasure of meeting him in person before he passed away. See next story.)

Story #3: Dave Thomas, Wendy's

Mr. Dave Thomas was an orphaned child. He says he never
knew who his birth parents were, but he was raised by the most wonderful folks in the world. He has done a lot for other orphans; we are
all God's children.

Dave Thomas did not finish high school. He dropped out in the
10th grade. As a teenager, he worked in a restaurant and really enjoyed
the food service industry. Back then, most restaurants were the full-
menu type restaurants: steak, pork chops, chicken, roast beef, fish,
hamburger, etc. However, he noticed that the majority of customers
seemed to like the fried chicken that was cooked with Col. Sanders'
recipe.

Dave and a few other folks came up with the rather radical idea
that you could have a successful restaurant that served only fried
chicken, mashed potatoes and gravy, green beans, baked beans,
macaroni and cheese, coleslaw, corn on the cob and biscuits.

Awww, come on, Dave, that won't work. Now, sure you can
have a fast food program built around hamburgers; Mr. Ray Krock had
already proved that with McDonald's, along with Burger King and
Hardees and some others, but just fried chicken? That will never work!

Mr. Dave and a few others proved that you *could* have a fried
chicken restaurant, and he was one of the original Kentucky Fried
Chicken franchisees with multiple, successful operations.

Then he came up with another rather radical idea. He felt that even
the very competitive fast food hamburger market could use another
franchise that focused on better quality (never frozen) hamburger meat
and real chicken breast sandwiches (not just chicken "parts" – remember the great ads "parts is parts" and "where's the beef?"). Many folks
said Wendy's, named after his daughter, would never work.

After 35 years, Dave Thomas decided to go back and finish high school. He did, and his class voted him "Most Likely To Succeed." Good choice; he owned about 4,000 restaurants at the time.

Story #4: Arthur Blank and Bernie Marcus, Home Depot

You know why Arthur Blank and Bernie Marcus started Home Depot? They got fired from their "regular jobs." They had to make a course correction. When Bernie called up a friend and told him that he and Arthur had been fired and what had happened, his friend said, "Congratulations, Bernie, you just got kicked in the ass with a golden horseshoe. Now go out there and start your own business." And that is exactly what they did. You may have heard of their business.

Incidentally, Arthur and Bernie wrote a book about the beginnings of their business, which they sell at Home Depot. Not surprisingly it's orange and it's called *30 Billion Dollars in 20 Years*. Now is that growing a company or what? The book costs only $19.95! Americans will buy anything for $19.95. Everything you see for sale on TV costs $19.95, or three easy payments of $19.95. (What is it? I don't know, but it's only $19.95 so let's get one.)

They opened up what we call a "Big Box Store." Home Depots look as if they have ten million dollars in inventory in the store the day they open up. I guarantee that the eighty percent / twenty percent rule applies to Home Depot, just like it does anywhere else. Eighty percent of their sales come out of twenty percent of their inventory. Then why don't they just carry the twenty percent of inventory that they know sells?

Well, because Home Depot's main draw is what they call a "big box." They've got just about anything. If you want a $3 hammer or a $300 nail gun, or some nails, come to Home Depot. They've got it. If you want to hang some wallpaper or fix a door, the "tradespeople" that the Home Depot hires as employees can show you how. Home Depot helped develop this market.

When Home Depot first started, only about 8 percent of people did "do it yourself" projects around the house. If a light switch didn't work, you called an electrician. If your sink was leaking, you called the plumber; for a leaky roof, the roofer. After 20 years of helping folks and holding seminars on how to "do it yourself," Home Depot has turned America on to the idea.

One other thing about business folks learning from other business folks. You know where they got one of their best basic ideas about marketing? Mr. Sam Walton.

When Home Depot first started growing, they would depend on special sale items to get customers through the door. The problem of managing inventory correctly for special sales was huge, however. If they featured a sale on leaf blowers in a store in Virginia, for instance, how many units did they need - 300, 700, 200? Sometimes they would run out, and sometimes they would create large amounts of overstock after the featured sale.

Mr. Sam advised them to get away from the special item sales, as Sears does, and instead, develop an acceptable competitive mark-up that gives great value for everything and be the low-cost provider on all items in the store all of the time. That way the customer doesn't have to decide - today we are going to this store or that store to take advantage of a special sale. They simply say, "We need to go to Home Depot or to Wal-Mart to get some things we need." And after they get you there, they know that you just might find some other items that you cannot possibly live without. (Put them in the shopping cart.)

Ever notice the main messages in Wal-Mart and Home Depot ads? They are value, low prices, *and* smiling, helpful employees. That was no accident - it was a course correction. Speaking of course corrections, I always liked the NASA story about the first man on the moon. Did you know that the first moon landing successfully landed within fifteen feet of the designated landing spot? Fifteen feet! Wow! However, the rest of the story is that they made approximately 86,000 course corrections from take-off to landing. Business, life and space exploration require a constant set of course corrections. Let's look back at business.

Chapter 13
Sellers

At Sunbelt and at most business brokerage firms, we have existing businesses for sale in all areas. Retail, service, manufacturing, distribution, food service, lounges, coin-op, liquor stores and others, in all sizes and locations. We also sell hundreds of franchise opportunities, new and re-sale. In addition, we sell main street businesses ($1 million in annual gross sales or less) and larger businesses ($1 million to $30 million in annual gross sales). One thing all of our listings have in common is that they have a seller, and they have a business story or history and a track record.

An existing business usually has the advantage of a track record at that location. It has survived three years or longer, and it has an established customer base, cash flow, and trained employees. It has established vendor relationships, furnishings and equipment that produce and distribute a product and/or service. The business also has a record of producing enough sales to pay the business expenses and provide for the owner's personal expenses such as his house payment, car payment, and feeding and educating his children.

However, if this is such a great business, then *why is it for sale*?

Why would an owner be selling a perfectly good business that is serving its purpose, providing a living for the owner and his family? What is wrong? A buyer always asks that question of a seller, and so do I as a broker.

In most cases, what's wrong is a human motivated situation. In other words, the owner is retiring; the owner or a family member is unfortunately in poor health; the seller or owner dies; is getting a divorce; is relocating; the owner has identified something else they would like to pursue in life and they can not do this business 8 to10 hours per day as well. Sometimes, the reason for selling is as simple as the owner being "burnt out" on the business after a while and wanting to do something different for a living. If he has only been open 6 months and he tells you he's burnt out – look out! However, real burnout after 5, 7, to 15 years is a very real reason for selling; it's like the seven year itch.

Just as we as homeowners sometimes move from one perfectly good house to another, there is nothing at all wrong with the first house; we just decide to move to another one. Sometimes we change jobs, change locations, change wives, change husbands, things just *change* as we go through life. Sometimes the change results in a need to sell a perfectly functioning business that has been providing for the owners, just as it is supposed to, but the owner wants or needs to sell the business.

That is life. But I always want to honestly know why the owner is selling. And the buyer also wants to know and has a right to this information also. If I wasn't completely comfortable with the seller's story about why he/she is selling, I would be very cautious about proceeding with a purchase. That is another reason why I want the seller to put his money where his mouth is and finance part of the purchase price.

What about the seller's *Exit Strategy*? Exit Strategy! What Exit Strategy? Small business owners don't have an exit strategy – their exit strategy is they plan to go down the highway, turn right onto the Interstate and head South. Most business owners are too busy running the day-to-day operations of the business to plan an exit strategy. Then one of the human driven changes comes up and the business and particularly the financials have not been prepared for an exit. That may be good, not bad, since you want the business to continue on its successful course with a seamless transition of ownership. The business continues, the seller quietly exits.

A franchise has the advantage of a recognizable brand name and a proven system of operations that has worked well in other locations. The market has responded well to the franchise's product or service, and the other franchise owners are successful and pleased with their investment in the franchise. A franchise is a partnership of sorts that establishes an ongoing relationship between franchisor and franchisee. Both parties have privileges, responsibilities and obligations to each other. Franchising has proved to be a very successful method of growth for many, many businesses in all sorts of industries. Franchising works and is a method of being in business *for yourself,* but *not by yourself.*

Now I am not trying to be blasphemous, but the very first and by far the most successful franchisor is Jesus Christ and the Christian Church. Jesus had started to grow His church by recruiting and training his franchisees (11 out of 12 of which were successful – what a great track record) and they started to spread his teaching and messages regionally at first, then nationally, then worldwide. His systems and trainings have changed the world. Even if you are not Christian, the very calendar you live by now was started by Jesus' birth, life and message; the world sets its clock by the birth of Jesus, the very hinge of history.

From a business standpoint, a franchise is a known name and a system of business operation that teaches you how to produce and sell your product and/or service throughout your market territory. It is a proven system of business success that is teachable, trainable, duplicatable, repeatable and that the marketplace responds to by purchasing your product or service. The individual franchisees are local owners/managers – a tactic to insure that the system is followed faithfully, allowing the success in one area to be duplicated and repeated in other areas.

Also a franchise may very well have some attractiveness to our buyer for the following reasons; the buyer came out of middle management of a big company. He or she was vice president of "X." They went to work everyday, and they managed successfully inside this box "X." The training people took care of training, the P.R. people took care of P.R., the R&D people took care of R&D and the finance people took care of finance.

When you buy a franchise they train you initially and then you go to work everyday, and you manage inside this box just as you did in your last middle-management job. Buying a franchise fits your comfort zone. The training people take care of training, the P.R. people take care of P.R., the R&D people take care of R&D and the finance people take care of finance.

Also, unlike an existing individual business, the financials are complete because the franchisor's systems are tied into the cash register, gross sales and the top line, not the bottom line, so that the corporate office can assist you in managing correctly and will monitor your success. Often times, they share in your success through royalty payments, so you both have a vested interest in your success and prosperity. You both have a vested interest in staying on the leading edge of the market trends in your industry.

Other good things that result from a franchise business relationship is that, unlike private individual business where the accountant and lawyer will not recommend that you buy the business because of Chapter 6 (the financials are not complete or accurate), the lawyer or accountant may very well recommend that you buy a franchise for several reasons. First, they have heard of the franchise, and they perceive it to be successful. Secondly, the financials balance, and "it's all in there." Thirdly, the UFOC, Uniform Franchise Offering Circular, is required by law for every franchise operation and gives the professional the information necessary for a basis to recommend that their client purchase that franchise.

Guess who buys a lot of franchises? Accountants and lawyers. Banks, also, may make a loan or finance the purchase of a franchise for some of the same reasons listed above. Up to 95 percent of franchises are still in business after 5 years. A franchise's success rates provide a very strong underpinning of value, which also corresponds with a lower risk.

A franchise re-sale has the advantage of a franchise's known name, system of operations, specific track record at that location, trained employees, existing customer base and cash flow. The financials should be accurate and complete, and you should develop a comfortable relationship with the selling franchisee or business owner and the home office or franchisor. Both relationships are very important to your success. Again, that brings up the additional question of why the seller is selling; a question whose answer we always want to feel comfortable about. I would also want to talk with some other existing franchisees of that franchise as part of my due diligence and always ask these further questions: "If you had to do it over again, would you buy this franchise? Are you happy with the franchise and are you making a living?" Even if I got all of the right answers, I would still require some seller financing in a franchise re-sale as I would in any other small business acquisition.

Sunbelt has partnered with one of our brightest, successful, young franchisees, Scott Evert in Minneapolis, to develop a specific program to assist Sunbelt offices with franchise re-sales. We have developed a program to build relationships with major franchisors to let us assist them when one of their franchisees wishes to sell. We are the only company that has an office in every city.

So if you want to sell an ACE Hardware store in Omaha, Nebraska; in Sacramento, California; in Ft. Worth, Texas; in Nashville, Tennessee, we have an office there to assist you. Former Speaker of the U.S. House of Representatives, Tip O'Neil, used to say that "all politics is local" – well, I say, "all small business is local, too."

Also, look in the mirror before you buy a franchise. Can you follow a system and do it their way? Or are you too much of an independent "cowboy" and only want to do your own thing? In the latter case, franchising may not be the best match for you. That is not to say that franchising is right or wrong. I am just saying that asking yourself that question will show you the best way to go with your own business decision.

Here's a good test. Were you an "A" student in school, a "B" student or a "C" student? If you were an "A" or "B" student in school you would be a good candidate for owning a franchise. "A" students usually excel at following directions and doing what is expected. "B" students can also be good franchise owner candidates. "C" students usually are not good candidates, because they don't like to follow directions.

"A" students normally do an excellent job in top management of a company or running a division of a company for "B" students who are often the President and do an excellent job of managing for the "C" students who probably *own* the company!

"C" students are cowboys, and they do better when breaking all of the rules, not following them. (Get these cows from Ft. Worth to Kansas City – how to get them there is up to the cowboy.) They are also survivors. Dave Thomas dropped out of school altogether (although he returned as an adult after succeeding), Thomas Edison never graduated, Henry Ford was not a good student, Bill Gates and Michael Dell dropped out of college, and Ted Turner? I bet he was a "C" student.

About two years ago, Sunbelt affiliated with a knowledgeable and experienced franchise marketing expert, Tom Miller, who knows more about business brokers selling franchises than anyone else on the planet. Tom is from the Phoenix area, and he has been a tremendous help to Sunbelt and other business brokers in understanding the sale of franchises. At Sunbelt, we "get it," and this year Sunbelt sold more franchises than all the other business brokers put together. We recently asked him to become President of Sunbelt Franchise Sales and Development.

When most folks think of Mergers & Acquisitions ($5,000,000 to $30,000,000 in annual gross sales) they think of investment bankers, stockbrokers and high-powered deal makers that you see on T.V. In our world, the real world of small business, a business doing over $1,000,000 in annual gross sales is a big business and one doing $20,000,000 to $30,000,000 is a *huge* business. Many business brokers do not handle $5,000,000 to $30,000,000 companies. This is what we call Mergers & Acquisitions or M&A deals. Even at the industry trade group, the IBBA, most folks handle "main street business brokerage." There is a group of experienced and professional brokers who are IBBA members that are also members of the M&A Source, and they focus almost entirely on the middle market of $5,000,000 to $30,000,000 plus.

While it has not been the primary focus of Sunbelt over the first few years of our franchise life, things have changed. Since many of our Sunbelt franchisees are very successful in "middle market" M&A deals, in addition to "main street" brokerage, we have opened Sunbelt Private Investment Banking, LLC, as an M&A division.

Bigger deals require financing. No buyer can write a check for several million dollars out of "Hip National." Oftentimes, banks are much more comfortable with a business doing $3,000,000 to $30,000,000 in annual gross sales. And in the larger transactions, many buyers invest some cash and some stock in acquiring the company. This is a whole different set of rules than with small business – this falls under football rules.

One of the best things that has happened to me and to Sunbelt (in addition to the wonderful and bright brokers who have joined Sunbelt as franchisees) is how we are becoming players on the M&A field. About half the calls my partner Dennis and I were getting from our franchisees as Sunbelt became the largest business brokerage franchise in the world with over 200 locations (currently we have reached over 300 offices), were regarding M&A deals. Our office owners were being contacted by owners of businesses that were doing $5,000,000 to $30,000,000 in gross annual sales, and they were looking for a broker to assist them in the sale.

The brokers would call me and say, "Ed, I have an appointment with a gentleman tomorrow who has a business that is doing $22,000,000 in sales. What do I do?" Of course I would say, "Go list it, we might sell it." Although this is an apt example, I know that selling a multi-million dollar company is a different business from main street brokerage.

Therefore, in 2000 I attended the annual IBBA meeting in Atlanta, Georgia, to learn more about M&A so that I could then add that to my broker-training curriculum. As fate would have it, there was a misprint on the schedule and a meeting that was supposed to be held on Thursday, taught by one of the top M&A instructors in the IBBA, Ken Hoganson from Chicago, was not being offered on that day, but earlier in the week - and I'd missed it. However, Sunbelt is always an exhibitor at the IBBA conferences, and Ken came by our booth. We have a little "AAA Road Map" in our exhibit that has red pins to show our locations around the country. Ken took a look and said, "Wow, you guys have certainly grown." I said, "Yep, the Lord has certainly blessed us, and we have a location in almost every city."

I then told him how sorry I was that I missed his course. I explained that I needed to train my brokers in handling bigger deals, but without losing our focus on the main street businesses. I said that we wanted to be the "Home Depot of Business Brokerage." If the buyer wants a $3.00 hammer or a $300 nail gun, it will be one stop - Sunbelt's got it! You want a small business, large business, franchise or franchise re-sale, one stop, call Sunbelt Business Brokers; we have the inventory, experience, professionalism and honesty to treat you fairly and help you find a business. I was on my soapbox.

We started talking, and being the wonderful teacher that he is, Ken said that he'd be glad to help us learn the M&A process and to assist us in any way he could. I'm pretty good at pushing the envelope and I always try to partner with folks who I feel are smarter than me and who I can learn from.

Then I asked him another question. About how many M&A deals do you handle in a year? He said "Eight to ten, on average." I said, "How would you like to do *a hundred?* If you join with us and head up our Sunbelt M&A division, teach us how to do our part, help us manage the sale and close the deal, we'll have something to offer that no one else has - the expertise of one of the nation's top M&A specialists and 1500-plus M&A broker agents in every city, all over America. Someone else can send out a letter; at Sunbelt we can send out a professional broker. We have the close relationship of a local brokerage office and the best M&A team in the business. From the Engagement Package, to the Confidential Memorandum, to the M&A appraisal, to the marketing book, to the growth plan, to the universal search for prospective buyers, to managing the showing, negotiations, letter of intent, due diligence, final bid and closing, we have it all!"

The new entity, Sunbelt Private Investment Banking, LLC (M&A Division), can work with the seller's team and the buyer's team of professional accountants, lawyers, bankers etc, to get the deal done in a way that is positive to both buyer and seller. Add that to main street brokerage, franchise sales, franchise re-sales, business financing, consulting and development and you have a full menu of business services. Call Sunbelt. This is the message behind our successful new venture.

Chapter 14
Valuation Methodology

Americans like to have an answer to the question, "what's the value?" of a business, car, home, investment, etc. Normally, we equate price with value when it comes to most of our purchases. At the check-out counter of the grocery store or at Wal-Mart, Kmart or Office Depot, the clerk runs the tag through the scanner and we pay the total price. For 95 percent of the things that we purchase, the price is the value. As I stated earlier when discussing negotiations, we, as Americans, usually either pay the asking price or we don't purchase the items.

In buying a house, we arrive at a value by looking at comparable prices of houses in that subdivision or market area based on square footage, features, location, amenities, condition, etc. However, we can come pretty close to arriving at market value based on comparable and competing properties - and remember that the banks are going to underwrite at least 90 percent of appraised comparable value. So, I can pretty well tell you what the value of the house is. One of the main things that upholds that value is the very fact that you can buy a house with only 10 percent down. Who cares what the house costs? What's the down payment and what's the monthly payment? If we can get you financed then we have a deal.

What is the value of a car for sale? As mentioned in an earlier chapter, the "blue book" will give you a market value of every type of automobile based on model, year, mileage, condition, etc, from both the retail and wholesale perspective. So, I can pretty well tell you what the value of a car is. And often the bank or finance company will finance a major part of the purchase. And nobody cares what the car costs, they care about the down payment and the amount of the monthly payments. To prove this, let's look at how they sell cars. "Low down payment, no down payment, $1,000 cash back, no payments until next year." The monthly payment has to be under $1,200 per month on a house and under $500 per month on a car. To keep payments under $500 on a car, they went from three year financing to four years, to five years, to seven years. When that didn't work because the price of the car kept going up, they came up with more ingenious plans. "We won't sell you the car, we'll rent the car to you (lease sounds better) – you don't own it, of course, but who cares – the payments are always under $500 and you had a low down payment." Now if the price of cars keeps going up, buyers will have to put a port-a-pottie in the back and finance it for thirty years while they live out of the back seat.

What is the value of a business? It depends. Now I can do a good job of arriving at a business's value based on several appraisal methodologies; Multiple of Earnings, Multiple of EBIT, Multiple of EBITDA, adding up the value of the hard assets plus 1-2 year earnings, discounted cash flow method, comparable business sales, etc., etc. However, no matter what method I use, there's no guarantee that *that* business will sell or that it will sell for that price.

You see there is no third party or bank financing to uphold 75 to 90 percent of the market value or appraised value or comparable value that I have determined. So first, I have to find someone who wants that business (that dry cleaner, that restaurant, that auto repair business) in that section of town. Then the market will determine if the business will sell and what it will sell for and at what price and terms. The buyer, the seller and the market drive the decision about the value of the business, and the market drives the price and terms of the deal.

In that one area a big business (publicly traded business) and a small business (Mom & Pop) are exactly alike. What is the value of a publicly traded company? It is not based on the value of its inventory, the value of its FF&E or a multiple of the EBITDA. The value of a publicly traded company is what the market (stock market) says it is, and that value is subject to wide and significant change. Although you bought shares of that company for $86.00 per share several months ago, that may have absolutely nothing to do with the share price and value of the shares therefore the value of the company today. It may be worth more; it may be worth less, as a lot of folks have found out over the past few years. Either way, it has a market driven value that may or may not have a direct relationship to valuation methodology.

A small business is just like that. I can do a very good appraisal of value based on the industry and the specific business. However, that does not mean that this specific business will sell, and it does not mean that it will sell for that price. One of the best approaches to value is to get an arm's length, legitimate, third party appraisal on the business before we take it to market. The appraisal serves as a "sanity check" as my friend Dan Elliott calls it, and it will also be necessary for any bank and/or SBA financing. However, ultimately, the market will determine value.

The market value is what a ready, willing and able seller (under no duress to sell) will sell for and what a ready, willing and able buyer (under no duress to buy) will pay for a business. Since both have knowledge of the market and value, the terms and conditions of the sale have to be agreed to by both buyer and seller.

When you add in the fact that I'm normally not dealing with a foolish buyer, nor do I want to be, and that I'm not usually working with a foolish seller, nor do I want to be, the market value works pretty well. The terms and conditions have to work for and be agreeable to both parties.

The buyer cannot put down more of a down payment than he has in "Hip National Bank" or that he can get; and the debt service on the balance, whether to the seller or to the bank, must be paid out of the business's cash flow. In addition the buyer must leave himself/herself enough to live on after all the business's bills are paid.

The seller has to agree to the terms and conditions also, or the business will not sell. Which means of course that if he does not sell, he still has to get up at 5:30 every morning and go open the dry cleaners, and the buyer is still burning through around $4,000 a month of his life's savings since he still does not have a job or source of income. A no sale is not good.

When we do arrive at a price and terms agreeable to both parties, that is the market value. And incidentally, a good business broker will add significant value to the deal for both the seller and buyer to help get to market value.

From the seller's standpoint, a broker can expose the business opportunity to hundreds of prospective buyers without employees, customers or competitors knowing that the business is for sale. The seller can go right on running the business and keeping everything profitable and attractive while the broker does the work of searching for a buyer. And managing the myriad of things that have to be taken care of in a business presentation and sale.

From the buyer's standpoint, how would you even find a good business that is for sale? There are no signs in the window saying "Business for Sale" or a multiple listing for businesses for sale that specifically identifies a business. Also, how would a buyer learn about "baseball rules" and understand how to look at the real value of a business, or figure out how to finance a business, or how to make an offer and negotiate without the assistance of a broker?

When your accountant advises you not to buy a business, or your lawyer advises you not to buy the business and your "friend" the banker won't lend you the money -that's great except for one little fact: you still don't have a job and you still don't have an income. Those professionals have not helped you solve your problems. And next month you have $4,000 less in savings at "Hip National Bank."

The business broker will help you find a solution to your problem, and it's a good solution. They will help you find a business and help you negotiate and buy it based on terms and conditions that work for you. If you wish to buy the business and do buy the business, you may have a job for life. You have the opportunity to grow the business and to possibly make more money than you would at a job, and you should have something of value to sell when you wish to sell.

The good and well-intentioned folks at the SBA, the Small Business Development Center and SCORE (The Service Corp of Retired Executives) actually know very little about "small business." As I stated earlier, these well-intentioned and sincere academics and retired big business executives do a great job with business plans and start-ups, but they seldom know anything about the real world of baseball rules (small business). They will look at the books of a dry cleaner that has been in business for 12 years and say, "I don't see how this is going to work. Look at the financials."

What do they mean it won't work? It has obviously been working for 12 years or his doors would be shut. The owner has been paying his payroll every Friday, his rent every month and his vendors on time or they would have cut him off. He's also paid his house payment, car payment, fed and educated his children or he would not still be there. The SBA folks, accountants and lawyers are all missing the forest for the trees. They would rather show you how to "start up" a business, do a business plan, keep good books and run it as they were taught in college classes and big business seminars.

They also never heard of owner financing and never understood the value of making a seller put "his money where his mouth is," the way you do in baseball rules. These folks are great football players, but this is not a football game.

The value of the business is what the value is to you as an owner or prospective owner. Will this business provide a living that works for you; if so, how much is it worth?

Following are some of the *Rules of Thumb* or *Field Formulas* that I've used successfully to arrive at a "ball park" value of a business. Then the terms and conditions of a specific business sale still have to be worked out between the specific buyer and the specific seller.

All of the formulas are based on some "multiple of earnings" or "true owner's net" based on the existing business and based on the most recent year's sales. Sales drive value, *sales drive value*! If there are no sales or low sales then the business has no value. If there is no top line then there can be no bottom line. Don't forget the 10-20 percent rule. It works very well for small business (under $1,000,000 in annual gross sales); 10 percent or less for middle sized businesses (over $1,000,000 in annual gross sales).

All formulas have to be appropriate to sales, however. The sales of a business - product and/or service - are the market's response to that business's product and/or service.

The furniture, fixtures, equipment and inventory should always be included in the sale at the "normalized" levels because the FF&E and that normal level of inventory produced the annual sales. They are part of the sale. When the new buyer closes the deal and goes to open the business the next day, the business should be ready for operations, ready for business as usual.

For the larger businesses (over $1,000,000 in annual gross sales), the financials are normally all-inclusive, and no cash is left out. The buyer would have to sit down with the seller and let him re-cast or normalize the financials to add back to the bottom line all areas of owner's discretionary cash flow, normally including the owner's salary, any additional family salaries that are paid to non-producing family employees, and all owner "perks" such as an owner's car, wife's car, children's car, insurance on the cars, health insurance, life insurance and trips that the family takes. Normally, you can also add back in depreciation, the debt and interest costs that will not be a cost to the new owner and also, any unusual "one-time" cost or expenses that will not reoccur.

When the recasting is complete, I will have a "true owner's net" that the business is providing the owner, and usually I will value that business at 3-5 times the "true owner's net." In other words, if the "true owner's net" were around $300,000, then the business would have a range of value from $900,000 to $1,500,000.

Some businesses may have a specific multiple but from a "Rule of Thumb" approach I would be comfortable with a 3-5 times multiple, following which specific negotiations would determine the final price and terms and whether it will sell or not.

For the main street businesses (under $1,000,000 in annual gross sales) the financials are not usually all inclusive. There may be owner's cash that is not depicted in the business's books and therefore cannot be recast or added back to the bottom line. I would use a "top line" approach to true owner's net in a small business. The following formulas also lend themselves to the real world of small business in that we'll have an *asking price* based on gross sales that is probably going to be considerably different than the *selling price*.

In small business, there are normally going to be "severe" discrepancies between what the seller wants and what the buyer can and will pay; however, the value is still determined using the gross sales as a basis. Out of the top line comes the bottom line. Here are some specific examples. I call them "Gross Sales Formulas."

1. *Retail Business (gift shop – Keystone mark-up):* 70% of gross sales would equal the asking price; 70% of the asking price would equal the selling price (approximately 49% of sales).

2. *Food Service (restaurants):* 60% of gross sales would equal the asking price, 60% of the asking price would equal the selling price (approximately 36% of sales).

3. *Service business (lawn care, janitorial):* 50% of gross sales would equal the asking price; 50% of the asking price would equal the selling price (approximately 25% of sales).

4. *Equipment Intensive Business (coin laundry, dry cleaners, printing company):* 100% of gross sales would equal an asking price (lots of equipment); and it probably will sell for approximately 70% of the asking price (70% of sales).

5. *Manufacturing (note - Americans like manufacturing companies; they carry the highest multiple):* a manufacturing company or machine shop may very well list for and sell for 100% plus its gross sales, especially if it has a "proprietary product" or a "patent" that the market ascribes value to (100% or 100% plus of sales).

6. *Liquor Store (inventory intensive):* there is not much of a mark-up in the liquor store business, normally only 15-22% on cost, so a liquor store will normally sell for the inventory, at cost, in the store at the closing, plus around two year's true owner's net. The true owner's net in a liquor store is not 10-20 percent; it is never more than 10 percent of gross sales.

7. *Convenience Store, with Gas:* I do not ascribe any value to gas sales (outside sales); gas is a commodity and the "big boys" control the price; when you think of it, that is the only business where you put the price "right out" on the street so customers

can see it before they pull in. If the store across the street is charging $1.28 per gallon of regular unleaded gas, you cannot charge a $1.50 per gallon and compete successfully.

The value of a convenience store comes from "inside sales." The mark-up on inside sales is normally 28-45 percent and in some cases, such as processed food semi-prepared on site such as fried chicken, nachos, hot dogs, popcorn, catfish, canned vegetables (no celebrity chef here!), perhaps even more. Also, there is great mark-up in fountain drinks and coffee. So if anywhere near 50 percent or more of gross sales in a convenience store come from inside sales, you've got a valuable store.

I'd value a convenience store at the 70%/70% formula based on inside sales; plus the gas inventory in the ground at closing, at cost, plus 5 percent of lottery sales if the store sells lottery tickets (the gross sales of the lottery are not included at all).

Any other business would probably fit the 70%/70% formula unless there are some unusual circumstances. Sellers always want as much as they can get, of course, and buyers would like to pay as little as they can. Somewhere in the middle is a fair deal that works for everyone; however, the sales price has to be appropriate to the sales. Not the value of the equipment, not the value of the inventory. If there are no sales, then there is no value.

General Motors has to have sales, Home Depot has to have sales, IBM, Lucent Technology, Nortel Network and Microsoft have to have sales. So why are the stock prices (market value) down on so many of these publicly traded companies, especially technology and computer related companies? Their sales are down, and sales drive value. Lucent Technology and Nortel have the same FF&E it had, the same inventory of products it had, the same patents, the same employees; what happened? Their sales are down, thus their value is down. (Now they have fewer employees.)

Another way to arrive at the real-world value in a small business arena is to look at the *opportunity value*. In buying a business, you are buying an opportunity to make a living for you and your family. The opportunity that you are buying just happens to be a business opportunity.

The best business opportunity may not be the perfect business. A perfect business is already running at 99.5 percent of its potential. You cannot improve the management that is already in place and there is no upside potential to increase the sales of the business. Also, if the business is perfect, the seller is going to want "top dollar" to sell.

The best business opportunities may very well be the ones that are chugging along at about 35-40 percent of their potential. You can buy it for the right price, add your learned and God-given talent to managing the business and run it up to 99.5 percent. That is where the best opportunities lie.

Here are some examples. I consider a McDonald's as a perfect business. It's already at 99.5 percent, and I do not believe that you could run a McDonald's restaurant any better than they do already. The store is always located in the best location; it's open from 6 a.m. to 12 p.m.; the food is good (may not be good for you, but it tastes good); the store is always clean and well lighted; there's sufficient parking; the friendly, well-trained staff usually takes your order correctly and does so quickly. Not to mention the marketing program that other restaurants would kill for. McDonald's partners with Disney, for goodness sake. The kids will beat you over the head to "go to McDonald's." I do not believe that anyone can improve upon the current business operations of a McDonald's. Therefore, you cannot make any more money than they are presently making. You cannot sell any more product than is already being sold from 6 a.m. to 12 p.m. A McDonald's restaurant normally does from $1,250,000 to $1,500,000 in gross sales, yet we are seeing even this success story operation go out of business in many locations for the first time. Here's why:

Food costs have gone up, labor costs have gone up, inventory costs have gone up, energy costs have gone up, property taxes have gone up, insurance costs have gone up, marketing costs have gone up - and they still have to sell a "Big Mac" for what they sold it for ten years ago. They still have to sell "Value Meals" for under $5.00. They cannot raise their prices, and they are maxed out in sales. So – to repeat - you cannot sell more product than they do already.

The investment in a McDonald's is approximately $1,500,000, and you might make $100,000 per year as an absentee investor. I do not consider that a good investment. However, it will work as a "Mom & Pop" owner managed business where the owner gets the $45,000 per year manager's salary and his wife gets the $36,000 assistant manager's salary. Now we return to how McDonald's started and the owner/operator franchisee puts in fourteen hours per day and makes the business work for them, for their family and for McDonald's.

Compare that business opportunity to this example. Let's take a hypothetical business that is not being managed to its full potential. The owner is tired, in poor health, playing too much golf, running around with his head waitress, hasn't changed the menu in years and is being chased by the IRS. In addition, if he has more than one location and he cannot manage more than one successfully, he has a problem. Or – another scenario - the owner dies, is getting a divorce, etc. Or this: Here is a closed restaurant. *A closed restaurant.* The seller may now owe the landlord $25,000 - plus in back rent. There is $200,000 in furniture, fixtures and equipment sitting inside. The equipment people are due money on their equipment. The present owner is gone, perhaps because of some of the poor management or circumstances mentioned above. The landlord and the equipment people are suing the present owner/tenant for funds due.

Why do you think that they haven't taken the equipment back out of this store? Two (real world) reasons: #1, what are they going to get for used equipment and where are they going to store it? Just as well store it in the restaurant. And #2, the landlord says, "Ain't nobody taking anything out of this store until somebody pays me $25,000 in back rent." We have what I call a "Texas Showdown." An unresolvable, never-ending dispute.

Now comes a buyer. He has only $25,000 in "Hip National Bank" that he can put down on a business. He needs to make a living for himself and his family. So, we put a deal together with a $25,000 down payment. Most of which goes to the landlord, less the broker's commission, of course, and a reasonable note with monthly payments due to the equipment folks. Nobody is quite whole, but everyone wins.

The landlord has part of his back rent and a new tenant who is going to stay and pay. The equipment people have something coming in for the used equipment and that's better than a kick in the britches. Even the previous owner (seller) comes out for the better - at least the harassing has stopped on the rent and the other business debts. They weren't going to get any money out of him anyway – he's broke. Even the lawyers aren't going to get paid on that deal. And that poor devil has enough problems already, between his ex-wife and waitress and all.

And guess what? The buyer, for a $25,000 down payment and a small note, just bought himself a business opportunity that if he works hard and manages correctly could make him at least $25,000 per year, every year for the rest of his life. He may even be able to make much more and then have something of value to sell when the time comes. That's a 100 percent return, plus, on his investment *every year* for the duration of his ownership.

Also, if he has a family, they would be able to eat at the restaurant. And if he hires some of his children and they steal food from him - so what. Since he has to feed them anyway, better to feed them at wholesale prices, rather than retail. (Now if any of the other employees take food, that's stealing; and that's not right.)

I maintain that if you can buy a business opportunity, existing business or franchise, and you can make back each year whatever amount you invested in down payment, then that is a 100 percent return on your investment every year. That's a good business opportunity. The total purchase price is not nearly so important as the down payment. Can you make a living out of the business after the down payment? That is what I call the ROI (Return On Investment) on a small business, and that is the opportunity's value. The opportunity to make a living for you and your family.

CPAs come up with different rules for ROI. They deduct a normal manager's salary for that business from my definition of ROI. They say that the manager's salary is not a part of their return. Okay for them, but I say, in the real world of small business, if you are the manager and that money goes into your pocket, then that's part of your return. It's your money and these are baseball rules!

Chapter 15
Protect Yourself; A Level Playing Field

A business deal needs to work for both the buyer and the seller or it probably will not work. There needs to be what I call a level playing field or a win-win situation.

Now both buyer and seller are taking a risk and to some extent they have to take a "leap of faith" in the sale. The buyer is risking his down payment or note or debt service, hoping he can make a living out of the business. The seller is risking that he may not get paid on the balance due to him, unless the buyer is successful in the business and pays him. Hence my theory that in business, $UCCE$$ $OLVE$ ALL PROBLEM$! If the buyer is successful, he will pay the seller and *everyone wins*!

Let's say that we have a business deal where, after negotiations, we end up with a purchase price of $100,000 with $40,000 down payment and a note back to the seller for $60,000 payable over 60 months at 7 percent interest.

Example: Selling Price: $100,000

-Down Payment: $40,000

Balance: $60,000 note to seller, payable over 60 months, at 7% interest

Assuming that the buyer only has approximately $45,000 in life savings or family money that he can put down on the business – who is running the largest risk, relatively speaking? The buyer or the seller? *The buyer.*

Should the buyer lose, he loses the down payment and the business assets. If he doesn't pay the seller and the seller forecloses, then the seller got the down payment and the business back, which he can re-sell. So even though they are both running a risk, normally the buyer is running the larger risk proportionately.

So how do you help ensure a level playing field between the buyer and the seller? Here are several important tips that work for both buyer and seller. Remember that if the buyer can't buy, then the seller can't sell. And I always recommend using former President Reagan's wise adage, *"Trust, but verify"*!

1. Find a broker that you feel comfortable with even though he may be an agent of the seller. He will not work against you as a buyer. Also find an accountant and an attorney with whom you feel comfortable. All of them are professionals and will assist you; however, the ultimate decision and responsibility will be yours.

2. Find a business that you like and would feel comfortable managing, providing that the seller or franchisor will teach you, assist you and train you how to manage the business successfully.

3. Review the sales, trend of sales and the owner's story about why he is selling. Study the industry in general. Is it a business

that has a product or service that has been and will be accepted by the marketplace? Ask the owner what the business is like and how much he is making. If his response fits the 10-20% rule, I'd believe him, as long as he is financing part of the sale. Ask him why he is selling and see if his reason passes your "gut feeling" test.

4. Make an offer based on terms and conditions that work for YOU, no matter what the seller is asking. The down payment must be what you can comfortably put down and the debt service must come out of what the seller says he's making and still leave you enough money to live on. You should buy a business based on what the seller is doing now, not based on the future potential of the business. You buy the business because of the potential, but you pay for what the business is doing currently (present day value).

5. The offer should be in writing with a $1,000 no risk, refundable deposit of money to be held by the broker in a Trust Account, totally and immediately refundable to you should you decide not to buy the business subject to any of the following contingencies.

6. Any offer should have at least these contingencies to protect you and the seller.

"This offer is contingent on the following:"

A. Buyer review and approval of the financials of the business.

B. Buyer review and approval of the terms and conditions of the lease.

C. Buyer review and approval of any and all "in place" contracts and/or agreements with employees, vendors and/or customers.

D. Buyer being able to obtain any necessary financing.

E. Buyer/seller agreement on an acceptable training and transition period for new management.

F. Buyer review and approval of any and all franchise documents and approval of the transfer by the franchisor (for a franchise).

G. Buyer/seller agreement on an acceptable industry non-compete agreement.

Note: Several of the contingencies are "walk away" clauses as big as a barn door for a buyer; however, that's the only way I'd recommend making an offer, subject to wide open due diligence and the ability to withdraw an offer for any reason if the buyer chooses to at this point of negotiations.

The terms and conditions of the purchase price should be clearly and simply stated. Try to keep the transactions as simple as possible. They can get complicated – all the more reason to begin with simplicity.

For instance, let's say that the seller is asking $250,000 for the business with $125,000 down payment. You may feel that is a fair asking price or a little too high. Most of the time the seller is asking too much. (Of course he is, he wants as much as he can get.) I don't blame him. He's selling his livelihood, his "baby."

If you had approximately $50,000 in "Hip National Bank" that you could put down on the business I'd suggest that you offer the seller the following:

$145,000 total purchase price with $40,000 down payment and the balance of $105,000 paid over 120 months at 7 percent annual interest. I would put the offer in writing with a $1,000 refundable deposit subject to the contingencies above and subject to due diligence. Give the seller three days to a week to respond to the offer.

Is the seller going to be happy with this offer? Absolutely not, and that's a little bit of an understatement. However, it is a serious offer and it's in writing with a deposit, which shows that you are a serious buyer and that you really want his business.

Is it your best offer? I hope not – never make your best offer at first. The seller will almost never take your first offer. I don't blame him; he thinks his business is worth more and it probably is. However, hopefully he will make a counteroffer (in writing) after some rather unkind remarks about your offer and perhaps some questions about your birth's legitimacy; however, we have "started the dance."

The counteroffer is almost always less than the asking price and may reflect closer to the selling price and terms that the seller will take. Now if there are other buyers who want the business and will pay more, you may have to adjust your offer considerably. If you are the only and best buyer, the seller has a decision to make. Does he want to keep getting up at 5:30 a.m. and opening the business or does he really want to sell it? We'll find out.

Now, when you are doing your due diligence, you may have a much better idea of what target of value, terms and conditions that your due diligence will verify. Many times without an offer to get a deal off center, you do all of your due diligence based on the asking price of $250,000 with $125,000 down payment. That's a "no sale" every time. For one thing you don't even have $125,000 down payment.

An offer in writing is the first step or first bridge that has to be crossed on this journey of buying a business. If we cannot get across this first bridge, the rest of the bridges don't matter.

Don't be afraid to make an offer that works for you. See what the seller responds with and be prepared to counter the seller's counter. Remember the "absolutes," which are: you cannot pay more down than you have or can get, and the cash flow of the business (what the owner says he's making), must cover the debt service and still provide a living for you and your dependents.

Hopefully, after one or two offers and counteroffers, you are in the ballpark of acceptable terms and conditions. Then you are ready to complete your due diligence. Why spend several weeks or months, hundreds or even thousands of dollars on accountants and lawyers, if we cannot even get in the ballpark on price, terms and conditions. Let's keep the horse in front of the cart. Let's cross this first bridge, or if not, move on to another business.

And remember that a lawyer's job and an accountant's job is to protect you – not to do the deal. They can never get in trouble for recommending "no;" they can only get in trouble for recommending "yes." Also be a little nervous about a lawyer who spends too much time "servicing" his clients. You might want him to work on a specific fee structure. (When I grew up in a small town surrounded by farms, we used to politely say that a bull was "servicing" a cow.)

One of the main reasons foreign buyers (new Americans) are buying so many businesses successfully is that they "make an offer" and "negotiate." For instance, let's say I list a convenience store with an American seller and let's say that seller is asking $300,000, all cash, for the store. My good American-born buyer looks at the business and says, "$300,000? That's too much" and he only has a $50,000 down payment anyway. Without negotiations, there is a no sale every time.

Now along comes a Korean-born new American. He looks at the store and the seller tells him he is asking $300,000, all cash, for the store. The Korean gentleman only heard him say one thing. "I want to sell." He offers the seller $45,000 cash. The seller is outraged and says, "Absolutely not!" A week later, he offers $82,000 cash, "Absolutely not!" A week later the undaunted buyer offers $82,000 cash and a small note back to the seller.

Three weeks later you go by the store, and the Korean gentleman is now the new owner. You know why? He made an offer. He started the dance. We can learn a lot from "new" Americans. And I'll bet you he didn't pay $300,000, all cash, for the store.

Chapter 16

Financing, Down Payment and Terms

Once you have located the business that you want and have developed a "gut feeling" that tells you this business would work for you, then you have to see if you can agree with the seller on terms and conditions of the purchase that work for you and are acceptable to them. The seller always wants more and you always want to pay less, but somewhere in-between is an acceptable middle ground.

The down payment is the most critical part of negotiations. Business brokerage is a "*down payment driven*" business. If we can work out an agreeable down payment, the rest of the terms and conditions can be anything that both parties agree to.

How much down payment ability do you have? A lot more than you may think. The main source of down payment is your savings or cash in the bank, personal assets, stocks, bonds, automobiles, and/or real estate that all could be liquidated and/or borrowed against to provide additional cash for a down payment.

Another often-used personal asset is your home. You may have a home valued at considerably more than the existing mortgage, and you may be able to borrow the equity though an equity line of credit or a second mortgage that is secured by your home or you may actually refinance your home.

Still other sources of funds are family and friends. Family and friends are what I call the "true venture capitalists" of small business. Looking for money from a "regular" venture capitalist for small business is almost as big a waste of time as for big business nowadays. I always tell my trainees, "If you ever find a venture capitalist, grab him, lock him in a closet and call me. I'll be on the next plane. I always wanted to see one of them." I've been hearing about venture capitalists ever since I got into this business over twenty years ago, but I have never actually seen one.

In small business, the venture capitalist is your family or friends. Your parents, in-laws, brothers and sisters, aunts and uncles, who care about you, trust in you, believe in you and will help you. I know that you never wanted to borrow money from your in-laws, but they just might be a great source of funds. Now of course, they never liked you very much, but since their daughter married you they'll help you out.

A word of business caution. This is a business deal and should be treated as a business deal. If you want to keep your family and friends, draw up a written note with agreed-to terms and treat this obligation the same way you do any other. Besides, from the lender's standpoint they want to help you and they want you to succeed and if they could earn a little interest on the side, why not?

A 401-K account may be liquidated if necessary or, under some unique circumstance, some of the money may be used for the purchase of the business without liquidating the 401-K. Now I know at first you say, "Oh no, that's my retirement and I have to pay a penalty to cash that in, in some cases, or, I'm saving that money for a rainy day." So what? If you don't have a job, you are already retired and it's raining.

How are you going to eat? You don't have a job and after all it's your money, it may need to be invested in your new venture.

The main thing that I always come back to is this. If you can put down however much in a down payment and perhaps make that amount back and possibly more each year for the rest of your life and hopefully have a valuable asset to sell when you do wish to retire, this puts the "risk" into proper perspective. And remember you've probably already put out hundreds of resumes for a job and no one has called you back.

Now, your home may be one of the best sources of funds; however, your house is different from the other potential assets to turn into cash. Mainly because your house is where you live and you do not ever want to lose your house. If you do, where are you going to live? In a tent? With your in-laws?

Should you decide to use your house as collateral for a home equity loan (provided your wife, who is absolutely petrified, will allow it), then that is okay by me. It is your asset and I believe the equity you have built up is also your asset to be used however you see fit. However, don't ever "cross collateralize" your house. In other words, you can use your home to borrow the equity, but do not ever use your home as additional security with a seller.

Here is what I mean, and this is very important. Let's say that you borrow part or all of the $40,000 down payment in our example against your home as equity and you use that as your down payment. I have no problem with that. However, the assets of the business that you are buying should secure the $60,000 note back to the seller. Do not also secure that $60,000 business note by adding the additional security of your home, no matter how bad the seller and particularly the seller's lawyer want you to. Just say, "My wife won't let me," because if she's smart, and women are smart, she's not going to let you. And remember, if she can't stop you, there is always Daddy.

Assuming one way or another we've put together almost enough of a down payment to satisfy the seller, we may still be a little short. If we are still just a little short, we may be able to run inventory down a little after closing to pay a short term note, or allow the seller to do that before the closing. Either way, it could provide another $10,000 - $15,000 depending on the business.

Another way to get the seller a little bit more cash within the first year of the sale (usually we think in terms of one year relative to income) is by agreeing to pay a small balloon payment or "catch up" payment after the business's busy season or after Christmas. You may be able to sell off some unneeded equipment or assign a portion of profits of a particular product or service as additional money to the seller for the year.

One way or another, through creative problem solving, you have to arrive at a total down payment that works for you and the seller. The terms and conditions on the note balance can be anything that works and is agreeable. You can do a straight monthly payment of principle and interest amortized at an interest rate over five years, seven years, ten years or whatever number of years is agreeable to you. This is not determined by an interest rate, or "prime rate," set by the federal reserve; negotiations set it.

I have done deals at 6 percent interest; interest payments only for 24 months, then the note balance is amortized at 6 percent interest over fifteen years with a balloon payment of the balance due after seven years. I have also done deals where there is no interest. Simply take the balance due and divide it by the number of months over which the payment is due. For instance, a $60,000 balance paid over 60 months (5 years) is $1,000. Nobody says you can't do that.

Also, I have had an agreeable deal between a buyer and a seller;

however, the business is headed right into the slowest time of the year for the cash flow of the business. Let's say that we're closing the deal on December 12th, with $40,000 down payment, and the balance due of $60,000 is payable after 60 months at 7 percent interest. The monthly payments would be $1,188.08, normally beginning 30 days after closing, January 12th.

However, both buyer and seller realize that the slowest time of year for this business is January, February and March. One way to make the deal more workable for the buyer and therefore increase his chances of success and at the same time increase the seller's chances that he's going to get paid (lower risk for the buyer and the seller) is to get both buyer and seller to agree to delay the start of the monthly payments for 4-5 months. Instead of beginning the payments on January 12th, what if we started the payments on April 12th?

Now with a bank, the first thing they would say is, "Hey, what about the interim interest?" What interim interest? If both seller and buyer agree, we'll start the same monthly payments as agreed, $1,188.08 per month for 60 months beginning April 12th instead of January 12th. Nobody says that you can't do that. Everything is negotiable, everything.

Some folks would call that "thinking outside the box." In small business negotiations, *there is no box*! There are no sides, no top, no bottom and no front or back. If there are agreeable terms and conditions to the seller and to the buyer, we have a deal.

And remember, if the deal works for the buyer, the buyer will be successful and the seller will get paid. That is exactly what they both want.

I have mentioned several times that, if a seller would not finance part of the purchase price, I would not buy it. That is absolutely true, and I tell all my buyers and sellers this fact. Sometimes I have a seller

when I first list a business for sale tell me he will not finance the purchase price because he is sick, or he is retiring or getting a divorce or he
is moving 1000 miles away. The market doesn't care about that any
more than the market cared that you invested most of your life savings
in Lucent, Webvan, or Worldcom.

The baseball rules still apply. Most of my buyers still have only
from $15,000 to $60,000 down payment ability, and the banks won't
make small business acquisition loans. So, probably the only way for a
seller to get the full market value of the business is for the seller to
finance the difference between the down payment and the balance due,
whether he wants to or not.

When we are able to get bank financing for part of the purchase
price, it does indicate a reassuring "second opinion" that this is a good
business. The very fact that the bank or SBA agrees to lend part of the
purchase price certainly gives you a comfort level that this is a business
that can pay off the debt service and make you a living. If he can, the
business broker will often try to help you get third party financing. Some
businesses you can get a bank loan on. However, the bank loan can
also bring up some other problems. If a bank makes a loan (SBA
guaranteed or not) they will want a "first position" security interest or
mortgage on the business's assets. This means that the seller's mortgage
or security interest, if any, will have to be behind the bank's security
interest.

Oftentimes the seller will say, "I don't want to be behind the
bank," to which I'll have to respond by explaining another of the rules
of nature, *"the big dog don't eat last"* and the bank is always the big
dog. That means, of course, that if the buyer is not successful, cannot
pay the bank and the bank forecloses, the only way for the seller to get
the rest of his money is to take the business back and pay off the bank.

Also, remember that small business is a relationship business.

When the seller lists the business, he may say, "I'm not going to finance anybody." Well, I wouldn't finance just "anybody" either. But what about lending these "nice people" some money once you have met them and developed a relationship with them. And after the marketplace has shown the seller what I've told him is true - #1 most real buyers cannot cash them out and most rich folks won't buy a business and #2 the banks won't lend because of the seller's financials, not because of the buyer's credit. And especially after the buyer has offered to put down everything they've got in a down payment. Once you have a *personal* relationship, then we can work on building the *financial* relationship.

Now in developing a financial relationship between the buyer and the seller, you have to remember that they both have their own perspectives. And out of their perspectives come their perception and their perception is their reality. Here is an example. Let's draw a curved line on the page like this:

*A. (Seller) →   )   ← B. (Buyer).

* note: I got this idea from an excellent seminar presented by Bob Davies, an outstanding motivational speaker and personal coach from California.

If I were to ask the seller (point A) whether this is a convex line or a concave line, he would say, "This is a concave line." "Are you sure?" I would say. Yes, he's sure and you know what? He's absolutely right. From the seller's perspective that is a concave line. The end points are pointing towards him.

Now I ask the buyer (point B), who incidentally is looking at the exact same line (however from a different perspective). I ask, "Mr. Buyer, is this is a concave line or a convex line?" He would say, "I can see it perfectly and it's a convex line, the end points are pointing away from me."

Well, they are both absolutely right. They are looking at the exact same thing but never from the same perspective. It is kind of like the relationship between a man and a woman. I think this came from the Lord's sense of humor. It's built in. We often are looking at the exact same thing, but *never* from the same perspective. And out of your perspective comes your perception and your perception is your reality.

"I like a big city;" "I don't like a big city." "I like cold weather;" "I don't like cold weather." "I think she is a pretty girl;" "I don't like her." "I think he is doing a great job;" "I think he is a bum." "I like the restaurant business;" "I don't like the restaurant business," etc., etc.

Now let's apply perspective and perception to our financial example:

$100,000 Selling Price

-$40,000 Down payment

$60,000 Note due to seller

From the seller's perspective and particularly from his attorney's perspective, he'll say, "I'm very worried about this buyer. He's only putting down 40 percent. We have got to have some *additional* security to make sure we get paid." That sounds so very logical from the seller's perspective.

However, from the buyer's perspective (assuming he's only got around $40,000 total life savings that he can get together, beg, borrow or steal), is this *only* a 40 percent down payment? Absolutely not! From the buyer's perspective this same $40,000 down payment is a *100 percent* down payment and commitment. It is a *total* commitment. It is all he's got to give.

So the seller and the seller's attorney insist that we need additional security. They are not going to take back "just" the business assets as security for the $60,000 note. They need additional security such as the buyer's house.

That just sounds so logical from a seller's perspective, but this is what the buyer hears: "I'm not comfortable that this business I'm selling you is worth $60,000 so we need some additional security." "What?!" says the buyer. "If the seller doesn't think that the business is worth $60,000, then why am I paying $100,000 for something the seller and his attorney do not think is worth $60,000?"

That is a pretty good question put in the proper perspective. Plus, when I tell the buyer he's got to also put his home up for security, I probably just killed the deal.

I do not blame the buyer. I would not put up my house to buy a business. It is just too much risk. In fact, if you look at what just happened, the "Risk-Reward" ratio got turned upside down on its head. What if the buyer got hit by a truck, what if the highway department digs up the street in front of the business for five months for a new water line?

The buyer could lose his entire down payment (life savings), he could even lose the business back to the seller and, if he pledges his home, he could also lose his house - everything in one fell swoop. That is too much risk and remember we weren't dealing with a risk-taker to begin with.

There are other ways to further protect the seller's security within the business.

1. Find the best buyer in the market by researching the broadest possible buyer base.

2. Make sure that there is a good training and transition period for new management that makes for a seamless transition.

3. Make sure that the terms and conditions of the sale are those

that allow the buyer to be able to "stand up under them" and be successful. So that he can and will pay his obligations to the seller and be able to make a living.

4. Require that a constant level of inventory be maintained at all times to insure the value of the security. Require a monthly sales or financial report for as long as the seller has a balance due to allow the seller to be helpful if the business starts getting off track – before we have a train wreck.

5. Require that all FF&E come under the security and that any and all "after acquired" or replacement FF&E come under the security.

These things help the deal work for both buyer and seller; therefore, they increase the security for each and also lower the risk for each. The continued success of the business works for all parties.

Chapter 17

The Right of Offset; The Teeth in Owner Financing

One other very important part of a relationship between the seller and the buyer is this: the *Right of Offset*. This means the right of the buyer to put teeth in his reliance on the seller's warranties and representation about the business including his verbal warranties and representation about the cash flow of the business.

For instance, every note we write in a Sunbelt transaction has written right across the face of the note from the buyer to the seller the following phrase:

"THIS NOTE SUBJECT TO OFFSET"

Now, that does not mean that the buyer can simply refuse to pay the note, because if he does, then the seller can foreclose and take the business back under the terms of the note and security agreement. However, there are two specific circumstances that allow offset.

#1 is *material misrepresentation*, which is a legal term for fraud, and #2 are *undisclosed liens* that impede the buyer's clean title to the business's assets that are not properly disclosed and/or addressed by the seller before or after the closing.

Let's look first at material misrepresentation. Say that the seller has represented to the broker and to the buyer that the business is doing $350,000 per year in annual gross sales and that he is making around $50,000 per year true owner's net. That fits my 10-20% rule, so I am comfortable telling you that the owner is telling the truth.

Now understand that this is the seller's representation, not the broker's. The broker does not warrant anything, just as the accountant doesn't warrant anything. Have you ever seen the front cover of a business's financial statement? The accountant has a disclaimer as big as a barn door, even if they have been doing the books for the business for several years. The disclaimer says (paraphrasing), "All of the information herein has been provided by the management" and "management has chosen not to comply with any of the rules of GAAP (generally accepted accounting practices) and therefore this accountant and this accounting firm makes no warranties and representation that this information is current, complete or accurate."

If this business owner's accountant who does his books every year won't warrant the information, then certainly the business broker won't either. Nor should they. The only person who really knows the whole truth is the seller; therefore, he's the one who should warrant that the information is true and correct to the best of his knowledge. And the buyer certainly has the right to rely on the seller's warranties and representations.

A note of levity: I've always liked the H&R Block ad that proclaims, "If you're audited, we'll go with you." Of course they will - it's not their problem. Sitting in front of an IRS agent, when asked, "Where did we get this information?" They will simply say, "The business owner right here gave it to us."

Oftentimes a buyer will want to meet with a seller's accountant. That's fair, but always keep in mind that what an accountant knows about a business is limited to what the seller tells him or turns over to him, no more, no less. This is important.

Unlike a lawyer, there is no client privilege with an accountant. In other words, if you were my lawyer, I could admit to you, "Yes, I killed that guy." My lawyer would say, "For goodness sake, don't tell anybody else that. We'll plead not guilty and let me do all the talking from here on out." My lawyer, no matter how horrendous the crime, cannot *ever* be a witness against me or he/she would lose his/her legal license. That is called client privilege.

The accountant does not have that client privilege. If he were made aware of unreported cash or inappropriate allocation of resources or unreported inventory or sales, he would then become a co-conspirator and could get into almost as much trouble as his client. He could lose his license. So most accountants have adopted Mr. Bill Clinton's "don't ask-don't tell" policy to small business accounting. They don't ask you about any information and you do not tell them; other than what you turn into them. Therefore, it always comes back to this fact. The only 100 percent reliable source of complete information about the business is the seller, and you certainly have a right to rely on his warranties and representation.

This reality has been blatantly exposed in the relationship between the Enron Corporation and its accounting firm, Arthur Andersen. We will all be witness to the accountant-client relationship as this debacle plays out in the court of law and the court of public opinion. However, these were audited financials, and small businesses seldom, if ever, have or need audited statements. Small businesses don't ever have reviewed statements; instead, they most often have compiled statements. That is why I keep referring to seller financing as the seller putting his money where his mouth is.

Now back to our example. The buyer has made his decision to

buy, based on the warranties and representations of the seller. Again, the seller expressed that his gross annual sales were $350,000 and he was personally making $50,000.

The buyer buys the business and takes over the management. He asks one of his key employees: "Mary, I understand that you did $350,000 in sales last year." Then Mary's jaw drops and she says, "$350,000? Who told you that? Man, last year was really slow. I'd be surprised if we did half that in annual sales." Wow! We've got a problem.

Now here are two scenarios to make my point. In the first scenario, let's assume my example of $100,000 purchase price with $40,000 being the down payment and a $60,000 on the note back to the seller. Good for you!

You go to your lawyer, after you get your head out of the toilet, of course, and tell him what happened, and the lawyer says, "Give me $15,000 and we will sue the bastards." Lawyers always seem to want $15,000. Sue them? You may not even be able to find them. If you are dealing with a crook, than you are dealing with a crook. But, in this worst-case scenario, you cannot find the seller and cannot get your down payment back. Thus, you may have just purchased the business for $40,000 *total*. Certainly you are not going to pay the balance due on the note. You will offset it because of material misrepresentation.

In a second scenario, let's say that the buyer was able to pay all cash, $100,000 at closing. He got the money from family and friends or the bank and of course the seller would always rather have cash.

You close and take over the business and say to one of your employees, "Mary, I understand you did about $350,000 in sales last year?" Mary's jaw drops, etc., etc., etc.!

Guess what? You just bought it. Even if you do sue the seller, what if you can't even find him? He's gone and the lawyer still wants

$15,000. That is why I like owner financing.

So, how do you know if the seller is telling you the truth about the business? How do you know that the cash flow is there; that there is not a significant environmental problem lurking that could put you out of business? How do you know that there isn't major competition or an industry change forthcoming that could put you out of business? How do you know that the equipment isn't ready to break down or that the employees won't walk out or that the main customers won't pull their business once you buy it and take over?

The best way to arrive at a comfort level and a level playing field is that the person who knows the answers to every one of those questions better than anyone is willing to invest in your success. And incidentally, in scenario #1, where the seller is lending you part of the purchase price, these problems almost never come up. If the seller is materially misrepresenting the business, or hiding something that could be a major problem, he won't lend you the money to buy it. Remember that we are not normally dealing with a foolish seller.

The second right of offset is provided to protect the buyer in an "asset sale" from undetected or undisclosed liens.

Here is where the sale of a business differs significantly from the sale of real estate. In real estate, if you have a debt instrument, it has to be in writing. That's the law. And it has to be recorded in the county where the property is located. That is the law. That is the very reason why, when the bank makes you a loan to buy real estate, they require that your lawyer (he's not really your lawyer, he's the bank's lawyer, but his or her fees are in the closing costs, so who cares) give the bank a title opinion and provide the bank with a title insurance policy on their first mortgage position.

The lawyer can do that in a real estate deal; he simply goes down to the courthouse and checks the records. You put down 10 percent, the bank lends you 90 percent and there is 100 percent of the purchase price right there on the table. The lawyer pays off any and all liens and records the new mortgage and certifies the title.

There is not a lawyer in Philadelphia, Texas, South Carolina, Florida or Tennessee who would *dare* give you or anyone else (including the bank) a title insurance policy on a business. Wouldn't touch it with a ten-foot pole. It doesn't exist. Cannot get it.

In business, we are dealing with Chattel Mortgages, UCC-I (Uniform Commercial Code) rules, and there is no law that says if a legitimate business debt is not in writing or that if it is not recorded at the county courthouse then it's not a valid debt or lien. Plus, there may be other potential lienable circumstances against the assets of the business that are not on any record. These could include accounts payable, withholding or other tax problems that have not yet surfaced, and lawsuits (business and personal) that have not yet been filed, or recorded, but are on their way. All of these examples could come up and bite you afterward because when the closing attorney or escrow agent searches the business title, they won't show up.

In scenario #1; $40,000 down payment and $60,000 due on a note to the seller – again, good for you. You have $60,000 to offset any undiscovered liens that impede the title. In scenario #2; $100,000 cash upfront at closing, you run the risk of having something show up that would impede or cloud your title. Too bad, you just bought it.

The positives of owner financing just make good common sense. This is the best way to build a solid foundation from which to take the "leap of faith" necessary to buy a business. Are there still some risks? Of course, but seller financing allows you to go as far as you can to lower or mitigate the risk and help you to keep a level playing field and get you to your goal line! And remember, when you get to your goal line and you buy a business, the seller just successfully got to their goal line and sold a business.

In a transaction where you can get an SBA or bank loan, the seller is signing warranties and representation to the United States Government that all the information is true and correct – so your "teeth" is an SBA loan.

Chapter 18
The Future from a Historical Perspective

Everybody thinks about the future. Some folks even worry about the future. Where will we be in one month, six months, two years or twenty years? Who knows? Certainly, I don't, and neither do you. We will never know what life has in store for us. But we have to do the best we can to plot and plan.

One of my favorite moments in one of my favorite movies, "Out of Africa," is when Meryl Streep's character recalls that Robert Redford's character had always said, "One of the reasons that the Lord made the earth round was so that we couldn't see too far down the road." There may be some truth to that. You never know for sure what lies down the road. You just have to trust the Lord or fate, if that's your preference, and prepare as best you can for today and for tomorrow.

A good friend, Jed Waterbury, once told me, "If you want to hear God laugh out loud, tell him that you have a five year plan." (You have to think about that one for a while.) Now that doesn't mean that you don't need to plan and prepare for the future. Only a foolish person would do that and you are obviously not a foolish person. You are reading this book! (You may have to think about that one for a while, also) However, usually the most reliable source of information about the future is the past. What will happen is best described by what has happened and what is happening now.

When John Naisbeth wrote his runaway best seller *Mega Trends*, the most interesting thing about all of his research is that it was a collection of facts about what was already going on. The future trends were a continuation of things that were already happening. It was just that most folks didn't see the trends because they were too busy with the present and trying to look into the future.

Using the *Mega Trends* method of looking into the future of business and the world of work, we can best project the future based on our recent past and what is happening now.

I do not foresee a time when big business will start rehiring folks by the tens of thousands or when job security will return to the point where you will stay with one company through retirement. I only see continued "rightsizing" as companies stay lean or get leaner, as continual improvements in technology and robotics eliminate the need for workers, and as foreign competition eliminates the jobs in the United States. However, you still have to have an income.

Now that's not all bad. There is a great deal of good in those realities. You just have to make the necessary course corrections in your thinking, perceptions and perhaps take that leap of faith and go into business for yourself, and thus provide for your own income and job security.

Americans are a fiercely independent and self-reliant people. We always adjust and adapt to the challenges we face. These next few years will offer great opportunities to small businesses that address a market need and provide a product and/or service that the market wants, needs and will pay for.

As a man or a woman, and as a provider, it is up to you to make the living for your family, and I believe with all my heart that owning your own business or your own "farm" will help you do exactly that. And I also believe with all my heart that normally an existing business with a proven track record of success or a franchise with a proven track record of success is safer than a start-up for all of the reasons we have talked about.

The main thing, as Nike says, is to JUST DO IT! Find the business that works for you. Look at the amazing opportunities that await you in your new world of work. Do your research on the marketplace and on yourself and get going. Focus and prepare and pray and you will find that a lot of folks will help you and I believe the Lord will help you. We all like winners. We like folks who take their talents and multiply them.

Now as I said in Chapter 1, I don't know much about life and business except what I have learned in the last 58 years and from the other lives that I've studied particularly as related to business.

And I have said throughout that, when it comes to small business, your life and your business are one and the same. What you do that affects your personal life, also affects your business life and what you do in your business life affects your personal life and therefore your family.

In general health and welfare, I will stop my recommendations at eat right, exercise moderately, get a reasonable amount of sleep (but not too much), don't smoke, love your children and grandchildren (they are God's greatest gifts to you) and try to make at least one woman or man happy; or at least one of them at a time.

If you were fortunate enough to be born in America, realize that we owe God and a lot of brave folks a lot for our freedom and opportunities and responsibilities. If you weren't born in America, get here as quickly as you can and you will be warmly welcomed as a new American. There is no other place on earth like it, and we are truly, truly blessed and living in the land of opportunity.

Use your learned and God-given talents to the best of your ability. Make sure that you get an education (formally and informally), but also make sure that you do not let your education get in the way of good old common sense. Also, remember what Will Rogers said, "Common sense is not as common as most folks think."

There have always been and will continue to be ups and downs in business and in life. Try to learn something from both and make good course corrections. When you think you are right, listen to your feelings and don't ever, ever, ever give up. Mr. Henry Ford is credited with the saying "If you think you can do something, or if you think you cannot do something; you are probably right."

Here is a simple poem that I keep on my desk.

PRESS ON

Nothing in the world can take the place of persistence.
Talent will not; nothing is more common than unsuccessful
*   men with talent.*
Genius will not; unrewarded genius is almost a proverb.
Education alone will not; the world is full of educated
*   derelicts.*
Persistence and determination alone are omnipotent.

-Author Unknown

So, although most of us have been given the tools, talents and the time, we have to provide the "sweat equity" or the work. We have to do our part to make our family farm or family business work. Long hours, hard work, more hard work and tough decisions are always worth the effort because your future will be provided for.

There are three stories found in the Bible's Book of Psalms that I recommend you review daily. Psalm 23: The Lord is My Shepherd; Psalm 127: Unless the Lord Builds the House the Builders Labor In Vain; and Psalm 128: May You Live To See Your Children's Children.

As my partners, associates and franchisees, and I have had the pleasure of growing Sunbelt, we have learned a lot about ourselves, about surviving in business and about businesses all across America. We've learned firsthand how difficult, exhausting, challenging, frustrating and exciting growing a business can be – we lost money for the first nine years. There is never enough time, never enough money, and good ideas (even great ideas) don't always work. Never give up, but try to honestly recognize when a course correction is due.

Keep your expenses down, as there is never enough money. Try to do what Dr. Thomas Stanley and Dr. William Danko suggested in the book, *The Millionaire Next Door*. Live *below* your means. Order the house wine. It's just as good and in 10 minutes it won't matter anyway, except that you'll have more money left. Use a debit card instead of a credit card and you won't be spending money that you don't have yet.

When we first started growing Sunbelt, my wife, Elaine, and Dennis's wife, Nancy, worked with us for several years, most often for no pay. Later Dennis's youngest son, Dennis, came to work with us to develop our technology department and later our Web site. In the November 2001 issue of *INC* Magazine, Sunbelt's Web site won a first place position in the annual "Best Web Sites In America" contest out of 800 business entries. Sunbelt has also been rated #1 in business brokerage almost every year since 1995 by *Entrepreneur* Magazine's annual ranking of the "Top 500 Franchises in America." Technology has contributed greatly to our success. Young Dennis is now Vice President of Technology at Sunbelt.

We later hired Dennis's older son David, a CPA with the Marriot

Corporation, now our Vice President and CFO, and my nephew Ben Pendarvis, who I rely on and trust as my assistant, and later one of my sons-in-law, Jason Martin, to run our call center. Jason had seven years experience in running call centers for banks and other big businesses. This brings up another very important point. Make sure that the family member/employee is a justifiable employee, not just a make-work family member. At Sunbelt, we strongly believe in family business and it has worked well for us. We enjoy it. Plus, sometimes your family will work for less than anyone else when you are just starting up!

Another thing is to always watch your overhead, always watch your overhead. I like to think that I'm frugal, but most other folks think I am cheap. Either way, I'm pretty good at squeezing a nickel. Here are a few business tips on keeping costs down. Never buy a new car. A slightly used car with a little warranty left is a much better value, and after a week it's a used car anyway. Never pay to fly first class. The back of the plane gets there just as fast and you never have heard of a plane "backing" into a mountain, have you? Stay at moderately priced hotels and motels. They usually offer a clean room and a free, healthy breakfast. (FREE- America's favorite word!)

If I have to pay over $70 per night at a motel, I feel as if I need to stay up all night watching TV and running the hot water, trying to get my money's worth. If you're by yourself and you drive, you can sleep awhile in your car (while not driving!) on a two day road trip, then check in after 6 a.m. in the morning and stay through that night for one day's room rent rather than two (take two showers, though). Don't tell anyone else you did that, but you just saved $70.

The one advantage that I got out of my Citadel education and U.S. Army Ranger School Training is the ability to sleep anywhere, anytime. That is especially helpful when you are flying at night, or overnight on the "red eye" back to Charleston from the West Coast. Also, if you're coming back from a trip and you're by yourself and you've got to leave on a very early flight in the morning, why not catch a ride with a friend to the airport the night before, sleep at the airport and save the $70 room fee and $25 cab ride? Folks look at you a little askance, but by early morning you get in line with everyone else and you have just saved $95.00. (And you might even write a book while you are spending the night at the airport.)

Don't ever borrow money if you don't absolutely have to. It's not that I don't like to borrow money, but it's the paying money back that is so difficult and unpleasant. If you don't pay folks back, they'll get difficult and unpleasant. Another thing is that if your true owner's net is 10-20 percent, often debt at 8 percent interest or more or factoring your receivables can eat up all of your profits. You are then working for the banks or the moneylenders rather than your family. If you do borrow money, pay it back as soon as possible.

I have seen debt break a lot of good businesses and good folks even though they worked hard and smart, myself included. In fact, one of the reasons I've always stuck with St. Phillip's Episcopal Church in Charleston, besides it being a beautiful place to worship and the mother church of the Episcopal diocese in South Carolina, is that during the mid 1980s they were about the only folks in Charleston that would take my check.

Incidentally, in 1729, a daughter of Joseph Pendarvis was married at St. Phillips and approximately 300 years later, my daughters were married there. I love weddings – they, like education, are a wonderful investment in your children.

Along these lines of investments of time and resources, I would also like to mention this. Always try to get up by 6 a.m. and watch the sunrise and start your day off with private time and prayer or your meditation of choice. Thank the Lord for your wonderful blessings and ask for His continued help and blessings in your life. This simple act is a major investment in the man or woman in the mirror.

I always begin my training sessions with a short prayer, and I ask my trainees to join me. I figure if you can pray before a football game, you sure ought to pray about some of the most important decisions that you are going to make. Such as, how you are going to provide a living for your family Now, other folks may not need prayer, but I sure do.

Don't spend so much when you have it so that you will have something when you need it. Eat out with your spouse at good, but moderately priced restaurants. Have a "date night" every week. It's important.

Invest in the best education possible for yourself and your children. Running and managing your family partnership is as important as running and managing your business. The more you know about the world and running a farm or business, the better. My sister, Lois, and brother-in-law, Tommy Harper, have four children that they raised with a lot of love, direction, encouragement and high expectations. Their oldest son, Tom, graduated from Duke University and Duke Law School; son #2, Mikell, graduated from West Point in 1995; daughter, Abney, graduated from UNC and attends law school at Tulane; and son #3, James, graduated from West Point in 2002. That is a strong focus on education and it will pay off in their children's success. My sister-in-law, Debra Bowen, is a smart computer programmer that put herself through college the hard way - at night. She graduated with honors, from the College of Charleston, with a degree in Physics, whatever that is. Her extra efforts in education have paid off.

Always give God back His 10% in whatever manner you feel is right and give it happily. Based on my experience, a 90% true owner's net to you and 10% to your partner is a great deal for you. Occasionally, you probably ought to give some of your 90% to the government, too. All in all, they spend it well and, of course, in the United States, the government is "us."

Always try to find a business *you like*. Now it's still going to be work, it's not play, but I believe that if you can ever line up what you like to do with what makes you money, then you have hit a home run.

When we opened a Sunbelt office in Minneapolis / St. Paul, with a good friend, Scott Evert, in 2000, we went out to supper in downtown St. Paul after the first day of training. You may or may not know this, but the creator of Peanuts (the Snoopy and Charlie Brown comic strip), Charles Shultz, was from St. Paul and he had recently passed away. Several statues of Snoopy decorated the downtown St. Paul area as a tribute to one of the city's favorite sons.

Now, I am not the brightest person in the world, but I have always been a pretty good "reverse thinker." It seems to me that sometimes I see things differently from some other folks. I think that I must have run into a lot of trees or fence posts when I was a kid. Here's what I imagined about Mr. Shultz.

Imagine him as a young man going home and telling his father, "Daddy, I think I am going to drop out of school. I have this great idea about drawing a comic strip about a dog. What do you think?" His Dad probably would have said, "Are you crazy? You have to get that education and a good job with a good company like 3M or something."

Thank goodness he did what he wanted to do and liked to do, and he enriched the world with his wonderful talent and the stories of his comic strip. It is still on the first page of the "Funnies" section as Classic Peanuts.

As we opened our pioneer office in Los Angeles in 1995, with our very successful franchisees Ron & Vickie Hottes, I had a thought. How about when Mr. Walt Disney first had to talk to a banker about his crazy idea. I can just picture this scenario. Walt walks in the banker's office all excited and says, "Mr. Banker, I've got a great idea. I am going to open up a family recreation park based on a theme of a little mouse named Mickey, and his girlfriend, Minnie. What do you think about that idea?"

I am sure the banker listened to him somewhat amusedly and said, "Eh, we'll get back to you on that one, Walt, but thanks for coming by." Now if he was lucky, the banker gave him a ballpoint pen with the bank's logo on it and a token to get out of the parking lot. Fortunately he persisted and persevered and did what he liked to do and he changed the world.

Just remember that whether you are working for yourself or you are working for someone else, you are always working for yourself. You are always self-employed.

Also remember that all business value comes from sales. This story is told by Mr. Brian Tracy, a wonderful businessman and inspirational speaker. Dunn and Bradstreet have done several surveys on what makes businesses successful and what makes businesses fail. You know what the single biggest reason for business failure in America is? *Low sales!* You know what the single biggest reason for business success is? *High sales!* Everything else is commentary!

Mr. Jack Welch, the very successful and now retired CEO of General Electric wrote a book that said many things I agree with, but two points in particular, that I would like to share with you. First, he said that if you were going to manage a business successfully in today's world, you have to constantly change the business to keep up with the constant changes in technology and in the constant changes in the marketplace or these changes in the marketplace and technology will pass you by.

When I was growing up, G.E. made refrigerators, stoves and light bulbs. Now they are one of the largest financial businesses in the world; that's where they make their money. They probably now "job out" or contract out the stoves, refrigerators and light bulbs.

The second thing that he said that I absolutely believe is that if you are going to manage a business successfully in today's world, you have to deal with the world *as it is*, not as you would like it to be. Now, is that good advice or what? He is a very smart man and many folks consider him one of the best CEO's ever; however, his prenuptial agreement ran out too soon.

Why don't small businesses keep better financial records? Why don't the banks make small business acquisition loans? Why don't colleges and universities teach classes on the "real world" of small business management? Why aren't there any $100,000 per year salary positions with job security in my town? Why don't stocks always go up? And why don't I have more specific information and direction in order to make a better decision?

I don't know the answer to these questions, but I do know this; you just *don't*. I cannot change the world, but I do hope that I can help some folks navigate the real world of small business and how to deal with it a little more realistically. Especially when it comes to your understanding of the real value of small business - *to you*. And most things that apply to life generally apply to business.

I will leave you with this simple philosophy. Try as best as you can to add value to every relationship and every situation that you find yourself in. Never burn bridges with relationships, especially those that affect your family members. If you ever get really upset with someone, especially a family member, sit down and write them a letter, explain and express your feelings completely, but never mail it. Try to see the other person's point of view. Don't ever expect anyone to do something that he or she doesn't think is in his or her best interest. Then you won't be disappointed in them.

Never miss an opportunity to attend a wedding, a funeral, a child's play or game or visit a friend who is ill. I know that you will be very, very busy, but always make time for family gatherings or these opportunites will pass you by (and you may need to borrow some money at some point). You will never regret the time spent with these activities in life, as they are the *most* important.

Then, do what you say you're going to do if possible and treat every person with respect; learn from folks who disagree with you even though they may be a pain in the derriere. You already know what folks who agree with you think. Let folks know how much you appreciate them, especially your family, friends and husband or wife.

Try your best to adhere to schedules, plans and goals as you set them out. It is good to challenge and push yourself; however, remember, "only Robinson Caruso can have all of his work done by Friday."

Take your business and your relationships seriously; however, don't take yourself too seriously. Every chance you get, listen to the words of wisdom and music of one of America's favorite poets, Jimmy Buffett. In the song, *"Changes In Latitudes, Changes In Attitudes"* he says: "If we couldn't laugh, we just would all go insane" and in *"He Went To Paris:"* "Through 86 years of perpetual motion, if he likes you he'll smile and say... some of it's magic and some of it's tragic, but I've had a good life all the way." Visit Margaritaville and have a "cheeseburger in paradise;" in real-ville, eat chicken or fish – it's better for you. Enjoy your life, the good and the difficult, as both are God's gifts. If we didn't have the hard times, we wouldn't know what the good times were. Be a happy person and you will share happiness.

Be friendly, even with your banker. You never know how long he'll have a job and he may become your real estate agent one day.

Best wishes, happiness and success and may the Lord bless you and keep you. Go into business for yourself and you just may have a job for life, the opportunity to make more money than you would working for someone else, and the opportunity to grow a valuable asset to sell and provide for your retirement. You will have built *your* family business or *your* family farm.

Also, remember that most big businesses started off as small businesses. Hopefully you will enjoy this journey towards success. Even enjoy traveling, as I do, if your market takes you there. But, with luck, your favorite place in the world will be your hometown and your own backyard. You just might surprise yourself and even your father-in-law. By the way, he actually likes you more than you might think because you are good to his daughter and you are the father of his grandchildren. And grandchildren are *the BEST*!

Respectfully,

Ed Pendarvis
Student-Teacher
Chairman and Founder of Sunbelt Business Brokers Network

Afterword

The Future of Sunbelt

Well, to show you how life mirrors art – guess what? We have recently sold my *baby*, Sunbelt Business Brokers. However, I sold it to the only folks that I wanted to – the Sunbelt franchisees, my friends and partners.

Over the years, especially as Sunbelt grew to a strong market position in our industry, several people and companies have been kind enough to express an interest in buying Sunbelt. I told them, "Thank you for your interest; however, Sunbelt is not for sale. It is my life's work."

When my friends and franchisees, Carl Grimes of Fayetteville, Arkansas and Dan Elliot of Houston, Texas, first approached me at the IBBA conference in New Orleans about selling Sunbelt, my reply was the same. "Sunbelt is not for sale, this is my life's work." Well, Carl Grimes said, "Ed, Sunbelt is my life's work also. We share the same goals and visions and we want Sunbelt to continue to grow and succeed."

Well, as Carl, Dan and I talked, I realized that this just might be an answer to a prayer. Sunbelt had gotten too big for me to run by myself, and Dennis, my partner, was focusing on other business. Dan said, "Ed, you were running the company like a small private business and it needs to be run like the big business it has become for us all to reach our potential." He was right – this last year Sunbelt did over $1 billion in transactions and generated over $78 million in commissions.

I agreed to sell Sunbelt with three provisions, 1) that the possibility of ownership would be offered to all Sunbelt office owners; 2) that I have an opportunity to buy back as much stock as anyone could own; and 3) that I have the opportunity to help run the company for the next five years. They agreed.

So Dennis and I put a price on Sunbelt that we considered fair and unfortunately someone had taught the steering committee how to negotiate a business deal and we ended up with an offer somewhere in between the asking price and the original offer. Then the due diligence committee came in and told me I had some warts. To which I said, "Warts? You think my warts are bad, you ought to see my abscessed tooth and hemorrhoids." Anyhow, we ended up with further negotiations and a fair deal where the seller was getting less than they thought the business was worth and the buyer was paying more than they would like, but a deal was accepted by all sides (with a lot of owner financing).

I believe the Lord sent me Bill Davoli, a business broker who recently joined our Charleston Sunbelt office, at the right time. Bill is a Citadel graduate and he has built a small business from scratch into a big business and sold it to a bigger company, then managed the big company's sale in a "roll-up" to a public company. His help in the Sunbelt sale to the Sunbelt Acquisition Company (SAC) was invaluable. Bill understands small business and large business and he served as the liaison between SAC, Dennis Sr., Dennis Jr., and myself. He justifiably had the trust and confidence of all parties (and believe me, there were a lot of parties to this transaction). The deal began closing around 10:00 a.m. on Tuesday, December 10th and we finished at the lawyer's office at 10:30 p.m. The attorneys did a great job and *we did it*!

On Wednesday, our new founding board of directors (Carl Grimes, Dan Elliot, Deb Moore, Dan Pedersen, Steve Rosen, Bill Davoli and myself) had its first meeting and we came up with three major objectives.

1. Focus on helping our Sunbelt offices to be more successful.

2. Focus on helping our Sunbelt offices to be more successful.

3. Focus on helping our Sunbelt offices to be more successful.

The new management team of Ed Pendarvis, President and Bill Davoli, COO, started immediately to formulate and execute plans as approved by the board. I sent out an e-mail to all Sunbelt office owners following the closing and here is an excerpt.

"Let me just end this letter by thanking each of you for your support, trust and assistance. Elaine and I feel that our business relationship and your friendship mean more to us than you will ever know. Building this company has been a labor of pure bliss as I have gotten to know each of you personally and all of your brokers over the years.

With your continued help and the Lord's continued help, we will be able to have a major positive impact on thousands of folk's lives as we help them sell or buy a business when it is the right time in their lives to do so. You are the experts, you are the knowledgeable brokers who know how to help solve problems and get the deals done. I am proud of all of you."

Best Wishes & Respect,

Ed Pendarvis